The Evolution of U.S. Military Policy from the Constitution to the Present, Volume I

The Old Regime: The Army, Militia, and Volunteers from Colonial Times to the Spanish-American War

GIAN GENTILE, JAMESON KARNS, MICHAEL SHURKIN, ADAM GIVENS

Prepared for the United States Army
Approved for public release; distribution unlimited

RAND ARROYO CENTER

For more information on this publication, visit www.rand.org/t/RR1995z1

Library of Congress Cataloging-in-Publication Data is available for this publication.

ISBN: 978-0-8330-9822-1

Published by the RAND Corporation, Santa Monica, Calif.

Preface

This report documents research and analysis conducted as part of a project entitled "History of United States Military Policy from the Constitution to the Present," sponsored by the Deputy Chief of Staff, G-8, U.S Army. The purpose of this volume is to provide the Army with a history of the evolution of the major laws that govern the Army that were written between 1898 and 1940.

This research was conducted within RAND Arroyo Center's Strategy, Doctrine, and Resources Program. RAND Arroyo Center, part of the RAND Corporation, is a federally funded research and development center (FFRDC) sponsored by the United States Army.

RAND operates under a "Federal-Wide Assurance" (FWA00003425) and complies with the *Code of Federal Regulations for the Protection of Human Subjects Under United States Law* (45 CFR 46), also known as "the Common Rule," as well as with the implementation guidance set forth in DoD Instruction 3216.02. As applicable, this compliance includes reviews and approvals by RAND's Institutional Review Board (the Human Subjects Protection Committee) and by the U.S. Army. The views of sources utilized in this study are solely their own and do not represent the official policy or position of the U.S. Department of Defense or the U.S. government.

Series Introduction

The current institutional arrangement of the Army, which comprises a Regular Army and two reserve components—the Army National Guard of the United States and the U.S. Army Reserve—has been the same since 1940. As a result, a conventional wisdom has developed that this structure is appropriate to the time and unchangeable. When debating the Army's size, appropriate roles and functions, and the laws required to authorize, empower, and govern the Army, U.S. policymakers often think about evolutionary institutional modifications and rarely question the underlying assumptions that led to this structure. It is easier to tinker with the existing Army than to consider fundamental changes to the Army's statutory foundation. This four-volume history of U.S. military policy argues that little about the Army's organization is unchangeable or constitutionally mandated, a fact that should give policymakers license to explore a wider range of options for the Army of the future.[1]

The National Commission on the Future of the Army (NCFA), which Congress established as part of the National Defense Authorization Act of 2015, is a case in point.[2] Congress gave the NCFA the mandate, among other things, to examine the assumptions behind the Army's current size and force mix. Despite this mandate, the

---

1 Prominent American military historical surveys are Emory Upton, *The Military Policy of the United States*, 4th ed., Washington, D.C.: U.S. Government Printing Office, 1903, pp. 83–84; William Winthrop, *Military Law and Precedents*, Boston, Mass.: Little, Brown, and Company, 1896; Marvin A. Kreidberg and Merton G. Henry, *History of Military Mobilization in the United States Army, 1775–1945*, Washington, D.C.: Department of the Army, 1955; Richard H. Kohn, *Eagle and Sword: Federalists and the Creation of the Military Establishment in America, 1783–1802*, New York: Free Press, 1975; Allan R. Millett, Peter Maslowski, and William B. Feis, *For the Common Defense: A Military History of the United States from 1607–2012*, New York: Free Press, 2012; I. B. Holley, *General John M. Palmer, Citizen Soldiers, and the Army of a Democracy*, Westport, Conn.: Greenwood Press, 1982; Eilene Marie Slack Galloway, *History of United States Military Policy on Reserve Forces, 1775–1957*, Washington, D.C.: U.S. Government Printing Office, 1957; Russell Frank Weigley, *Towards an American Army: Military Thought from Washington to Marshall*, New York: Columbia University Press, 1962; Russell Frank Weigley, *History of the United States Army*, New York: Macmillan, 1967; Russell Frank Weigley, *The American Way of War: A History of United States Military Strategy and Policy*, New York: Macmillan, 1973; U.S. House of Representatives, *Review of the Reserve Program: Hearing Before the Subcommittee No. 1 of the Committee on Armed Services*, Washington, D.C.: U.S. Government Printing Office, February 4–8, 18–21, 1957. A reference guide for the legislation behind the military policy can be found in Richard H. Kohn, *The United States Military Under the Constitution of the United States, 1789–1989*, New York: New York University Press, 1991.

2 Public Law 113-291, National Defense Authorization Act for Fiscal Year 2015, December 19, 2014.

NCFA elected not to reconsider the Army's statutory authorities and responsibilities and instead focused on ways to refine and improve the existing force. The commission's published report argued that the nation has "one Army" and a "traditional military policy" for sound "historical, cultural, legal, operational, and strategic" reasons.[3] By using this phrasing, the NCFA reinforces the idea that a coherent and constant "traditional military policy" has governed the Army from the earliest days of the Republic. The NCFA's report offers 63 recommendations for such things as improving Army training and readiness, refining the mix of forces and capabilities, and improving personnel management. Yet none of the 63 recommendations calls for a reconsideration of the fundamental laws that authorize, empower, and govern the Army, or the Army's three-component construct.

The notion of a coherent and constant *traditional* military policy stretching from the earliest days of the Republic to today is, however, a myth. U.S. military policy evolved substantially between the writing of the Constitution and 1940, and very little has changed since. Indeed, the term *military policy* was not used in the United States until the late 19th century, when Brevet Major-General Emory Upton introduced the term to Army thinkers. As used by Upton, the term *military policy* connoted matters pertaining to the U.S. Army, such as the laws that govern the institution and the policies for wartime expansion. Today the term continues to refer to Army matters to the exclusion of the other Services. The term *traditional military policy* first appeared in the 1940 Selective Service Act.

We highlight the etymology of the term to underline the fact that today's military policy is not the result of a coherent tradition but rather the distillation of over two centuries of debates and compromises between various competing interests, many of which arguably reflected the political and cultural debates of the day at least as much as the need to meet the military requirements of the nation's security. For each generation since the writing of the Constitution, ideology, political culture, and institutional momentum have limited the discourse on military policy and constrained the range of options available for serious consideration. Indeed, the current force structure is strikingly different from anything the Framers of the Constitution imagined. Although the notion of doing so was once considered anathema, the United States now entrusts its national security in part to a standing, professional force—its Regular Army, augmented by two largely part-time yet highly professional standing reserve components. Once organized to defend a growing nation protected by two oceans, the U.S. Army today is postured to deploy globally on very short notice.

One important example of how the use of the term *traditional military policy* can be misleading is the current Title 32 of the U.S. Code, which states that "In accordance with the traditional military policy of the United States, it is essential that the strength

---

3 National Commission on the Future of the Army, *Report to the President and the Congress of the United States*, Arlington, Va., January 28, 2016, p. 1.

and organization of the Army National Guard and the Air National Guard as an integral part of the first line of defenses of the United States be maintained and assured at all times."[4] Yet the National Guard's role and status, and the laws governing it, have evolved considerably over time and cannot be regarded simply as a continuation of the 18th century method of producing military ground forces by "calling forth" various types of colonial militias, as the term *traditional military policy* implies. In fact, there is little "traditional" in the evolution of military policy.

One of the more fundamental developments explored in this series of reports is the subtle yet significant shift in the constitutional basis upon which the Army is built. Simply put, the Constitution includes one clause that empowers Congress to "raise and support Armies" and two other clauses that provide for "calling forth the Militia" of the states, as well as the authority to organize, arm, and discipline them "as may be employed in the Service of the United States," for the purpose of executing the laws of the Union, suppressing insurrections, and repelling invasions. The formulation assumed—accurately, at the time—that the states maintained their own militias or at least the means to raise them, even through conscription. Thus, the basic formula was for the country to rely on the "raise and support Armies" clause to maintain a small, standing federal army, but otherwise rely on the states and their militias to provide the bulk of the Republic's fighting forces. The militias evolved, as did their relationships with federal and state governments. In brief, the missions and personnel of militia referred to by the Constitution are not the same as the missions and personnel of what eventually became the National Guard. The evolution of the latter had less and less to do with state governments (and the Constitution's militia clauses) and more and more to do with the federal government (and the "raise and support Armies" clause).

In this four-volume series, we seek to establish an authoritative foundation for the debate over the best design for the future Army force. Drawing on archival research of primary sources and a survey of the historical literature, we trace the emergence of the laws that govern the Army today. This history has policy relevance because it shows that change in military policy is both possible and perhaps appropriate. When senior political and military leaders design Army force structure, thinking should not be constrained by such historically and politically loaded terms as *traditional military policy*. When imagining a future force, senior political and military leaders should recognize that current statutory foundations could be further defined and refined to enhance the Army's ability to meet the nation's dynamic security needs.

Figure S.1 depicts the evolution of U.S. military policy across a timeline from 1775 to the present. Along the top of the figure, we provide the strategic context across five periods—emerging America, the Civil War and the war with Spain, the World Wars, limited wars, and the Global War on Terror—as well as the nature of the Army in these periods. Along the bottom of the timeline, we highlight the specific historical

4 U.S. Code, Title 32—National Guard, Section 102: General Policy, 2012.

Figure S.1
The Evolution of U.S. Military Policy, 1775–Present

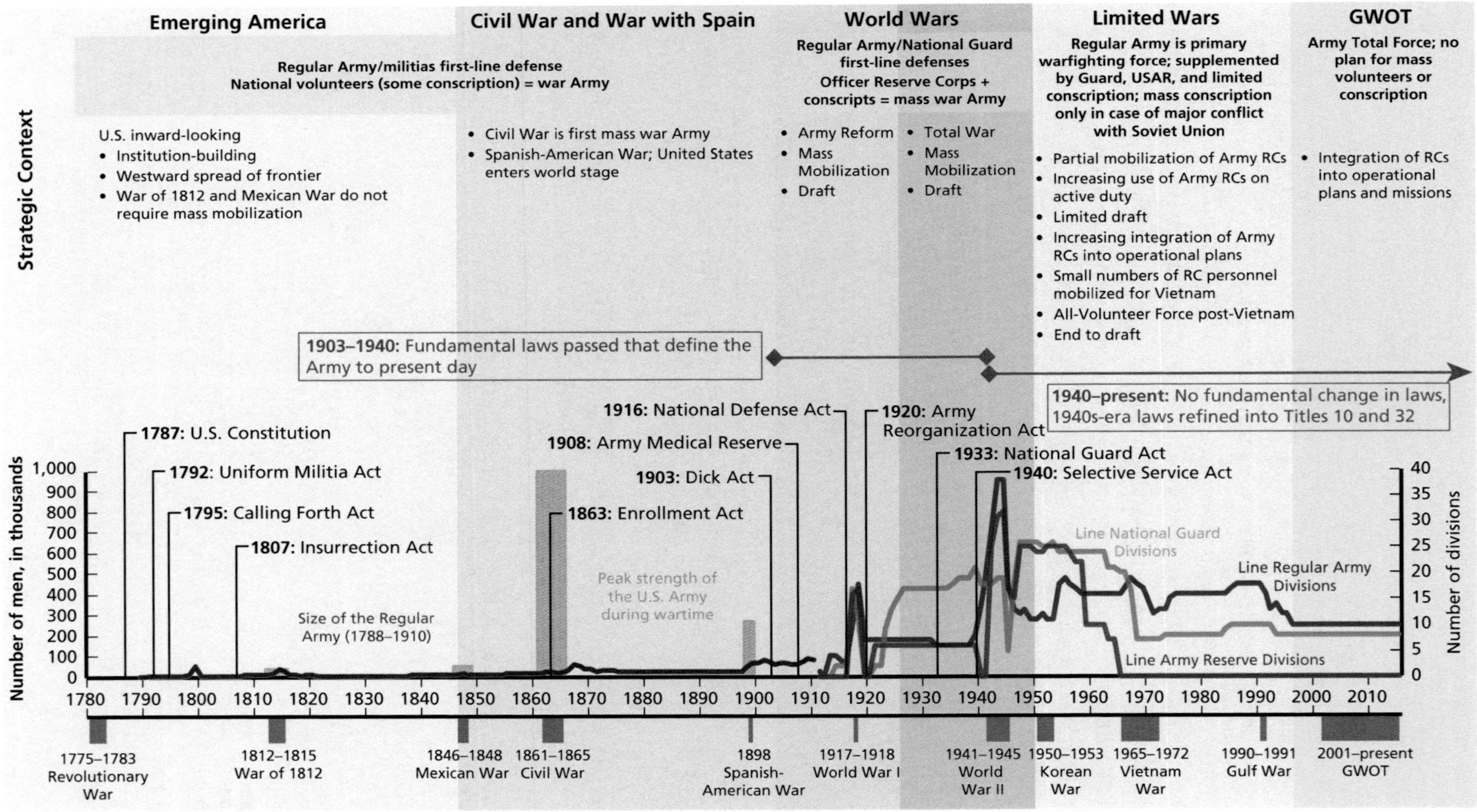

NOTES: USAR = U.S. Army Reserve; RC = reserve component; GWOT = Global War on Terror.

RAND *RR1995z1-1*

context in these periods, including the major wars fought and the size of the Army as it evolved over time in terms of the number of soldiers (the left axis) and the number of divisions (the right axis). In the middle of the timeline, we highlight the major relevant pieces of legislation that affected the evolution of the Army. The laws passed between 1903 and 1940, like the laws bearing on military policy before and after, reflect the debates and challenges of a particular historical period that differs greatly from the security environment that the nation confronts today. The laws nonetheless have remained virtually unchanged since 1940, as indicated in the figure by the thick red lines, despite significant changes in the geostrategic environment and the nation's increasing global interests and commitments.

In Volume I, *The Old Regime: The Army, Militias, and Volunteers from Colonial Times to the Spanish-American War*, we trace the history of military policy from the colonial era through the Spanish-American War. This period is critical for understanding the genesis of the basic structure of today's Army and the various factors that informed that structure. For a combination of strategic, cultural, economic, ideological, and political reasons, the Republic decided against establishing a standing army large enough to handle a major conflict and instead relied on a variety of mechanisms for raising volunteer units and marshaling state militias to expand or augment the Army. There was a basic split between proponents of a professional federal force, who judged the state-provided militias as militarily ineffective and too often contributing to an irresponsible loss of American lives, and those who opposed or feared the idea of a standing federal force (and its costs) and wanted to rely on "the people at arms," i.e., the citizenry organized by the states as militia units. The result was a compromise—an increasingly professional yet small Regular Army and various kinds of volunteer forces and state militias upon which the federal government would rely when the Nation needed to field a much larger force. However, authorities and responsibilities between the federal government and the states regarding the militias were not well established, nor were any mechanisms to ensure that the militias were ready and well trained when "called forth." Nor was there any mechanism to ensure the militia forces from one state were organized, trained, and equipped like the forces of another state to facilitate their integrated employment.

Problems with military effectiveness and recruitment contributed to an evolution in the militia system. The state militias shifted over the course of the 19th century from a colonial-era compulsory force (more compulsory in some communities than others) of all able-bodied white males between certain ages to entirely volunteer units with ambiguous relationships to their state governments. States that provided funding to their community militias tended to exercise more oversight and control. The compulsory militias were all but defunct by the time of the Mexican War (1846–1848), and volunteer militias provided much of the bulk of the Union Army during the Civil War. Postwar, those same volunteer militia units—increasingly referred to as "National Guard"—began to receive more support from state governments (with some federal assistance) and evolved into today's National Guard. Still, their status remained vague, as did their relationship with the federal government and the Army. Mobilization remained largely ad hoc, and the country still lacked anything resembling the large and rapidly expandable militaries fielded by France and Germany in 1870.

The Spanish-American War (1898) was a major turning point. The nation mobilized much as it had for the 1846 Mexican War, using a combination of Regular Army troops, volunteers from states and territories, and state militias. Small Regular Army units were rapidly assembled from small outposts distributed mostly throughout the central and western states, where they rarely trained for any contingencies other than fighting any remaining Native Americans who had not been pushed out of the way and onto reservations and preserving the local peace. Because of concerns associated with the constitutional limitation of militia use beyond the nation's borders, some individual state militia units voted to decide whether they would be mobilized (federalized) for the war with Spain. Some agreed, and some declined. If the unit agreed, the militia unit was brought into federal service as a volunteer unit. Other units were raised purely as federal volunteers (e.g., Teddy Roosevelt's Rough Riders), bypassing the state militia system entirely. A large-enough Army was eventually raised under the "raise and support Armies" clause, but profound problems were identified across the force. All elements of the Army were largely unprepared for fighting as larger organized units. Many units were ill-equipped, the Army's logistical capabilities were inadequate for deploying and sustaining forces overseas, and the tiny Medical Department was overwhelmed by infectious diseases that spread quickly through the ranks. The Army's difficulties were so bad that, in spite of winning the war, the Secretary of War was dismissed.

The volunteer militia units varied considerably from state to state, with little consistency in terms of readiness, quality, equipping, tactics, etc. Interoperability among or between them and the Regular Army was far from assured. There was, moreover, no established mechanism for generating forces to serve overseas for lengthy periods of time. This became a problem when the United States found itself occupying the Philippines and then fighting an insurgency there. Now the nation required an expeditionary capability, and it needed a force large enough to sustain a long-term occupation.

Heavily influencing the military policy of the late 19th century and early years of the 20th century was the maturation of the National Guard as a political force. Influential members of the Guard in 1878 created a lobby group, the National Guard Association, that enjoyed considerable sway with the public and in Congress. Because of the Guard's political influence, military policy debates and the relevant legislation passed in the 20th century often represented political compromises between the National Guard and the National Guard Association, the Regular Army and War Department, Congress, and the President.

As we shall see in Volume II, *The Formative Years for U.S. Military Policy, 1898–1940*, the challenges associated with the Spanish-American War stimulated new Secretary of War Elihu Root to promote reform through a series of laws beginning in the first few years of the 20th century. These laws, the most important among them being the Efficiency in Militia Act of 1903 (also known as the Dick Act of 1903, named for Ohio Congressman Charles Dick, who simultaneously served as chairman of the House Militia Affairs Committee; president of the National Guard Association; and commander of the Ohio Division, National Guard, with the rank of Major General), swept aside the Uniform Militia Act of 1792. They recognized the National Guard (i.e., the state volunteer militia units that had emerged after the Civil War), needed to be organized, trained, equipped, and disciplined along the lines of the Regular Army. This was the first step toward what in 1970 would become the Total Force Policy, and it added substance to the federal government's relationship to the National Guard, including both funding and regulations. These laws and subsequent legislation passed in 1916, 1920, and 1933 made the Guard largely a creature of the federal government, but one that still retained at least a formal connection to state governments—a dual status that in previous decades would have been anathema to Guard advocates. The laws of this era also established what would become today's Army Reserve, starting with a medical reserve cadre and the Reserve Officers' Training Corps. These congressional initiatives improved the Army's ability to expand and gave the Army access to trained specialists of the sort that were in short supply in the war against Spain. Although the new legislation greatly facilitated the nation's relatively rapid and orderly mobilization for World War I, some problems remained, and new ones emerged. Like all previous defense laws dating back to the Constitution, the legislation passed in 1916, 1920, and 1933 represented compromises. Debates of the era focused on how best to meet the nation's security requirements given a still deep-seated resistance to the idea (and cost) of maintaining a seemingly large standing peacetime Army, especially in light of Southern memories of federal forces being employed to enforce civil rights during Reconstruction. There was a grudging acceptance that, in the wake of the Spanish-American War, America required something more robust than the 19th century state-centric method for Army expansion; but there was little agreement over the details.

Volume III, *Another War and Cold War*, covers the period from 1940 to 1970 and examines how the Army, while retaining the basic legal underpinnings established by 1940, evolved in light of the radically different security requirements associated with the nation's emergence as a superpower and the need to maintain forces overseas and to rapidly respond in support of alliance commitments. Through this period—marked above all by the wars in Korea and Vietnam—there were vibrant debates regarding how best to generate the required forces, as well as different attempts by policymakers to balance military requirements with political concerns. These experiences led ultimately to the development of Total Force Policy, which was an effort to eliminate the need for conscription, except in special circumstances, and to further professionalize U.S. military forces.

Volume IV, *The Total Force Policy Era, 1970–2015*, covers the period from 1970 to 2015, from changes to U.S. military policy that resulted from the Vietnam War through years of persistent conflict following the September 11th, 2001, terrorist attacks. In spite of significant changes in the strategic context during this period, the fundamental laws underpinning U.S. military policy remained largely unchanged. Military policy did evolve through Army policy changes and congressional appropriations, although these generally reinforced the existing tripartite structure of the Army. To deal with the strategic, domestic, and financial constraints of the 1970s, the U.S. Department of Defense adopted the Total Force Policy. In its implementation of the new policy, the Army adapted the force mix within its three components to, when combined, fulfill the demands of war plans. The Regular Army was designed predominantly around combat forces to meet contingency timelines, while increased reliance was placed on support forces in the U.S. Army Reserve and Army National Guard to augment the Regular Army and to serve as a strategic reserve. Additional combat forces were maintained in both the U.S. Army Reserve and Army National Guard. Total Force Policy endured even as the nation's strategic circumstances dramatically changed again at the end of the Cold War.

Volume IV also discusses how the demands of persistent conflict since the 9/11 terrorist attacks have led to increased use of individuals and units from the reserve components. For example, as of June 2017, about 25,000 of the 542,000 soldiers of the Army Reserve and Guard are mobilized (federalized), with many serving in Afghanistan and Iraq. Army access to its reserve components has been simplified, and the American public largely supports their regular use, even in combat zones of the type experienced since 9/11.

Contents

Summary

American military policy has its origins in 17th and 18th century American political culture, especially the experience of the colonial period and the Revolution. American colonies, drawing on British traditions and memories of the English Civil War, saw standing professional armies in the hands of a monarchy as a threat to liberty. They preferred to rely for their local collective defense on community militias, which obligated nearly all adult (white) men to be prepared to serve. This consensus view persisted even after a few American leaders, including George Washington, concluded from the militia's poor record during the French and Indian War (1754–1763) and the Revolution that militias alone were inadequate and that the young nation also needed a professional standing military.

In the years immediately following the Treaty of Paris (1783) and during the debates over the Constitution, Federalists such as Washington, Alexander Hamilton, and Henry Knox argued for creating a Regular Army. Because they understood or shared the concerns of most Americans about standing armies, they did not seek a large force but instead insisted on a professional Regular Army and a "well regulated" militia subject to some federal oversight, in order to ensure a modicum of standardization and readiness. They would later be described as the "professionalist" camp.

Opposing them were critics of the Constitution who preferred to rest primary responsibility for the nation's defense on state militias. The compromise between these two groups was constitutional language that enabled Congress to "raise and support" a Regular Army (the "armies" clause) and "provide for calling forth the Militia" for the limited uses of enforcing the nation's laws, quelling rebellion, or repelling invasions (the "militia" clause). All understood that the Regular Army would be as small as possible, while the states were expected to maintain their militia forces.

Time and experience obliged the new Republic to modify its policies somewhat: The Native American threat grew through the 1790s, prompting Congress to increase slightly the size of the Regular Army but also to pass new legislation designed to clarify the roles of the Army and the militias of the states and set guidelines for the militias. The most notable of these laws was the "Act to provide for calling forth the Militia to execute the laws of the Union, suppress insurrections and repel invasions" (also known as the 1792 Uniform Militia Act), which reaffirmed that able-bodied white male citizens, 18 to under 45 years of age, shall be enrolled in their local militias. The law did not, however, establish a relationship between the Regular Army and the militias of the states, nor did it establish mechanisms for obliging the states to meet federal guidelines regarding issues such as training and equipment, which remained in the hands of the states.

By the 19th century, three distinct kinds of militias had evolved:

- The first were the "common" or "compulsory" militias, which were typical of colonial America and, by and large, the kind of militia to which the Constitution refers. These had the advantage of being a tried approach to mobilizing manpower that was familiar to all and for which state and local governments already had laws on the books. The disadvantages of common militias were that they were limited to three-month terms of service and could not be deployed beyond national borders.
- We refer to the second type of militia as "state-formed volunteer" militias; these were generated by state militia systems for federal service. They could be enlisted for longer terms of service, although, like the common militias, they were generally organized under the militia clause of the Constitution, which introduced a significant degree of uncertainty about their legal status and whether or not they could go abroad. The states generated these volunteer militia units generally in times of crisis, when directed by the federal government to furnish a specific quota of fighting men.
- We refer to the third type of militia as "state-sanctioned volunteer" militias. These were purely voluntary organizations formed by men who enjoyed participating in the military life on a part-time basis. States did not raise these militias, although states did give them charters, worked with them, provided them some support in the form of money or surplus equipment, and sometimes relied on them. This type of militia existed during the colonial period and throughout the 19th century.

The War of 1812 revealed the structural weakness of the militia system outlined by the Constitution and subsequent laws, such as the 1792 Uniform Militia Act. Mobilization was slow and inefficient, and short terms of service left the Army struggling to maintain a sufficiently large force structure to defend the nation against both foreign and domestic threats. The common militia had the additional problem of having to stop at the nation's borders, unhinging plans for the invasion of Canada. To compensate, the Army had to recruit directly into the Regular Army and rely on voluntary militia units. Another problem was that Washington's reliance on state militias—common or voluntary—exposed the Army to the problem of having to depend on state governments, some of which dragged their feet because of their opposition to the war.

Following the War of 1812, Secretary of War John C. Calhoun sought to improve the nation's defenses by calling for an "expansible" professional army, a skeletonized or cadre force that was top-heavy in officers at the head of half-strength units. In time of war, individual soldiers would be recruited into the units, thereby quickly doubling the size of the force. Calhoun thought this a more efficient approach than calling up militia units led by less experienced officers or creating new Regular Army units. He wanted to base the expanded army entirely on the Constitution's armies clause and apply the militias of the states to local duties.

Calhoun succeeded in bringing the Federalists' professionalist approach to Army expansion into the 19th century, but otherwise failed to affect the policy itself: The Regular Army shrank to a bare minimum after the War of 1812 and once again had to rely on ad hoc combinations with state militias. The anemic Regular Army was at least becoming increasingly professionalized, thanks in large part to the influence of the United States Military Academy at West Point, which had opened in 1802. Professionalization paid off in the Mexican War (1846–1848), in which West Point graduates markedly contributed to the Army's overall success. The Regular force was, however, too small to meet the military requirements of the war alone. Congress had to scramble to mobilize a combination of common militias (whose short term of service and inability to cross the Mexican border limited their utility), state-formed volunteer militias, and the independent state-sanctioned volunteer militia units. All of these types of militias, the federal government understood, would organize themselves or be organized at the state level and then be handed over by the states for federal service in Mexico under the armies clause. In any case, whereas the War of 1812 exposed some of the weaknesses of the existing military policy, the Mexican War validated it: A small yet relatively professional force paired with an ad hoc coalition of militia units prevailed.

The outbreak of the Civil War prompted a comparable mobilization, with Congress and the President at first scrambling to mobilize militias of various types, including large numbers of common militias, which were of immediate use in the early days of the war but fell into disfavor because of their short term limits. Congress came to favor volunteer regiments.

A major increase in the federal government's power to generate military force in wartime was the 1862 Militia Act, by which the federal government appropriated the states' right to draft men per the 1792 Uniform Militia Act. The act instituted a federal draft that, if applied, would have bypassed the state systems and brought men directly into federal service. The reason was clear: It had become problematic to rely solely on the states to generate wartime armies, or at least for the scale that major modern wars required. A year later, Congress issued a similar law, known as the Enrollment Act, which reiterated the federal government's right to draft, but also added that all men between 18 and 45 now constituted "national forces," an idea that suggested a national, federal reserve for the Army.

After the Civil War, the Regular Army once again shrank, and there was a renewed debate over military policy. On the pro-militia side, a major development was the rise in prominence of state-sanctioned volunteer militia regiments (the kind not raised by the state militia system) that increasingly styled themselves as a "National Guard." These militia cum Guard units, though local governments often used them for local civil disturbances, were increasingly interested in formalizing their status as a reserve to the Regular Army and part of the nation's defenses, although they zealously defended their association with state governments and resisted federal control. They aspired to missions greater than constabulary work or strike-breaking. To promote their interests, they formed the National Guard Association in 1878, which in later years would play a major role in military policy debates. In the professionalist camp, Brevet Major-General Emory Upton took up the banner after the Civil War. He updated Calhoun's expansible model and, drawing on his personal observations of European army mobilization systems, argued for pairing the Regular Army with a federal reserve force. Upton's scheme would have dedicated the Guard to precisely the kind of local role it wanted to transcend. Upton's writings had little effect on military policy during his lifetime, and it should be recalled that few Americans in the second half of the 19th century believed the country required a military that was any different from what they already had, let alone one fit for land warfare against a major European power.

The next great crisis for the Army was the Spanish-American War (1898). Once again, the ad hoc system that relied on a coalition between a small, professional Regular Army and an ad hoc combination of militia/Guard units proved adequate, in the sense that the United States won the war handily. A variety of fundamental problems, however, exposed the limits of the system and suggested that enough had changed—the nature of warfare, America's new security requirements, and the need to project and sustain forces overseas—to warrant reform.

Acknowledgments

Throughout the project, our sponsor, Timothy Muchmore of the Army Quadrennial Defense Review Office, provided very valuable input with drafts and a deep commitment to this history of U.S. military policy, for which we are very thankful and deeply indebted. Sally Sleeper, director of the RAND Arroyo Strategy, Doctrine, and Resources Program, provided us with encouragement and sound advice along the way. We are indebted to RAND Arroyo director Tim Bonds for providing some additional assistance at a crucial point in the archival research process. RAND's Terry Kelly was also hugely influential in the earlier stages of the writing of this history. For this specific volume, we are indebted to the reviewers of this report: Stephen Vladeck, professor of law at the University of Texas at Austin; Rob Citino, senior historian at the National World War II Museum; and Tom McNaugher, former RAND Arroyo director. For the digital version of this volume, we thank Tim Strabbing, Grace Rebesco, and Michael Bricknell of Rowan Technologies for their hard and most excellent work in producing the digital publication. Many thanks also go to Tamara Elliot of the U.S. Senate Library, who was always there for help in acquiring primary documents and for providing expertise on American legislative history. Anne Armstrong and Ryan Trainor at the National Guard Museum provided the research team with access to a trove of primary evidence. At the Hagley Museum and Library, we appreciate the assistance of Roger Horowitz and Lucas R. Clawson. Gail Kouril and Betsy Hammes, both senior librarians at RAND, provided very helpful assistance and suggestions for the research done on this project. Lastly, we thank RAND's James Torr for his expert editing and Todd Duft, Mark Hvizda, Marcy Agmon, Martha Friese, Jessica Bateman, Yamit Feinberg, Patrice Lester, and Lisa Sodders for shepherding this report through the publication process.

CHAPTER ONE

Introduction

In this volume, the first in a four-part series, we trace the roots of U.S. military policy in colonial practices and describe its evolution during the formation of the new Republic, paying particular attention to the framework established by the Constitution and the immediate context that informed it. We then explore the evolution of military policy as the nation struggled to generate the forces required to respond to the crises of the 19th century. Our aim is to provide the reader with a thorough and accurate appreciation of the antecedents to the Army that emerged in the 20th century, the force with which we are familiar today. Among the differences between the Army during the formation of the Republic and the Army of today are the nature and role of militias and the variety of assumptions about their relationship with the federal government and the Regular Army. The 18th and 19th century Republic largely relied on state-generated militias that would come under federal control to meet its security requirements. The nascent nation's military security requirements, especially from foreign invasion, were modest, while its ability to fund a Regular force was even less so. In response, the Republic gambled that it could accept the risks associated with maintaining only a small professional force that, with time, could be expanded with the help of state governments, upon whom the lion's share of the burden of generating forces fell. The system, though sloppy, inefficient, and not without risk, worked for expanding the Army against the type and scope of threats faced. The country won its wars in the 18th and 19th centuries, with the exception of the War of 1812, which the United States could congratulate itself for having survived.

One of the more striking features of U.S. military policy as it emerged in the 18th century was the weight of culture, ideology, finance, and politics, which combined to form a consensus hostile to large standing armies and favorable to reliance on state militias and the "citizen at arms." Some dissenters, among them war veterans and prominent Federalists such as George Washington, Henry Knox, and Alexander Hamilton, thought little of militias and advocated for a professional standing army. But they were realistic enough to know that, at most, the new Republic would be willing to accept and fund a small yet professional force that could provide a solid core around which a larger force might be built. They hoped for some mechanism to ensure that the militias be at least "well regulated," meaning that they would have to meet some standards that would ensure at least a modicum of quality and interoperability. What they got instead was the compromise articulated by the Constitution and put into practice by Congress in the first decades of the Republic's existence: a (very) small, professional force, with the local militias retaining pride of place, and with a federal government relatively powerless to regulate them or to impose standards.

Moving forward into the 19th century, new crises prompted adaptations, largely to address the inadequacies of 18th century methods for creating and expanding adequate ground forces. As we shall see, the reliance on state militias repeatedly proved problematic, though ameliorated somewhat by the evolution away from the compulsory militias that predominated in the 18th century in favor of various kinds of volunteer militias. Nonetheless, mobilization remained an ad hoc affair, and the general level of readiness was deplorable. The federal government was able to field large armies, as it did during the Civil War, but not without having to pass new laws that, among other things, appropriated for the federal government the power to conscript men, something previously only the states could do, and not without a great deal of delay and waste—in lives and in treasure. The experience encouraged new proponents of the professionalist school—most notably John C. Calhoun and Emory Upton—to update the arguments once made by Washington and his peers. It also encouraged post–Civil War proponents of the volunteer militias to argue for formalizing their status and integrating them more explicitly into the nation's defense capabilities.

A word about race: One of the unfortunate peculiarities of American military history during the 18th and 19th centuries is policymakers' views on race. Race weighed heavily on American thinking about the kind of military force it needed, and for what purpose. There were concerns about arming African-Americans and about ensuring sufficient militia strength to deter or suppress slave revolts. Slavery, of course, also informed thinking about states' rights and the balance of power between federal and state government. Much of this history is beyond the scope of the present study; however, we feel it important to remind the reader that, for a significant portion of U.S. history, a major feature of American discourse on military policy—the ideal of the civilian-soldier and of a nation defended by an armed citizenry rather than a professional force—applied to whites only. The militia laws discussed here that ostensibly made military service the universal burden of all male citizens of a certain age either explicitly applied to whites exclusively or left the distinction unsaid because it was understood that African-Americans were excluded. The 1792 Uniform Militia Act, for example, explicitly applied to whites only.[1] Blacks and other nonwhites were not, in fact, always excluded, everywhere, but for the most part they were. Those in politics who envisioned the nation at arms generally did not imagine nonwhites to be part of that. Only during the Civil War, in March 1862, did Congress remove the word

---

1 U.S. Statutes at Large, An Act to More Effectually to Provide for the National Defense by Establishing a Uniform Militia Throughout the United States, Second Congress, Session I, Chapter 33, May 8, 1792 (1 Stat. 271).

"white" from the militia statute, presumably to encourage African-American participation in the Union effort.[2] Afterward, racial policies varied, with black militias existing in some places, some of the time.[3] Only in the 20th century did it become widely understood that laws relating to recruitment and conscription applied to all races. For this reason, we have inserted the word *white* in parentheses where relevant to indicate that certain laws or policies applied exclusively to whites.

---

2 U.S. Statutes at Large, An Act to Amend the Act Calling Forth the Militia to Execute the Laws of the Union, Suppress Insurrections, and Repel Invasions, Approved February Twenty-Eight, Seventeen Hundred and Ninety-Five, and the Acts Amendatory Thereof, and for Other Purposes, Thirty-Seventh Congress, Session II, Chapter 201, July 17, 1862 (12 Stat. 597).

3 John K. Mahon, *History of the Militia and the National Guard*, New York; London: Collier Macmillan, 1983, p. 108.

CHAPTER TWO

The Antecedents of U.S. Military Policy: Colonial Times to the Constitution

The U.S. Constitution, the foundational law of the Union, contains numerous provisions for national defense. It gives Congress the authority to "raise and support armies," to "maintain" a navy, and to "provide for calling for the militias of the several states" to deal with internal threats to security. It makes the President of the United States the "commander in chief" of the land and naval forces, as well as the state militias when called to federal service. In the early years of the Republic, therefore, the U.S. Constitution provided the legal means for the nation to build military forces for national defense. But exactly how the nation would build its military forces, beyond the general authorizations provided by the Constitution, remained unclear. For example, what size should the standing Regular land and naval forces of the nation be? Should the Regular Army be large or small? How should it be organized? What should be the roles and expectations of the state militias in national defense? In what ways, if any, should they be brought under federal control, and at what expense of state authority? These types of questions, along with many more, challenged the new Republic in the first decades after constitutional ratification. The way in which the new Republic answered them was shaped by history, culture, and financial limitations, just as the Constitution itself had been. In particular, the American experience with colonial militias and their antecedents from Great Britain, along with a strong fear of standing forces, profoundly shaped how the American people and their elected political leaders chose to provide for the common defense with military forces. In this chapter, we trace that experience from the earliest days of the first English colonists landing on the eastern coast of new continent, through nearly a century of living under British colonial rule, through American resistance to that rule and ultimately revolution, and examine how this history influenced the writing of the Constitution.

Colonial Militias

English settlers in the 17th century brought to their first colonies in Virginia and Massachusetts an ideology and political culture grounded in centuries of tradition and popular interpretations of England's recent civil war.[1] Historically, the bulk of England's military power came from community militias, in which all male residents between certain ages obliged to serve when called upon, but usually with clear limits regarding the length of their service and how far from home they could be sent. The country's monarchs also maintained standing forces, but these were viewed with suspicion, and their expense made large forces economically and politically difficult to maintain. The bitter experience of the English Civil War encouraged the view that large standing armies in the hands of a central authority placed local freedoms in jeopardy, especially if the authority and local communities adhered to different religious confessions.

In 1636, the Massachusetts Bay Colony's governing council, following centuries of English precedent, established America's first regiment of militia by bringing together a number of disparate local militia companies from Salem, Boston, and their surrounding areas. The regiment was responsible for the primary security requirement of the era: defending settlements from Native Americans and conducting offensive operations against them. Militia service at that time was compulsory for virtually all white males from the age of about 16 to 60. As we shall see, the compulsory militia would remain a principal feature of America's defenses for more than a century, and its decline in favor of volunteer militias in the 19th century would mark a critical evolution.[2]

During King Philip's War in 1675 between New England settlers and Narragansett Indians, local "councils of militia" drafted men into militia companies, either to defend villages and towns or to go on offensive operations against the Native Americans. As recent scholarship has shown, the men drafted into new militia companies did not represent the broader society. Instead, the militia councils tended to target young men without families and indentured servants, who usually had minimal standing in the communities. The death of these types of men would be less of a burden to the

---

[1] On the early modern English roots of the American militia system, see Mahon, 1983, pp. 6–13.

[2] Kyle F. Zelner, *A Rabble in Arms: Massachusetts Towns and Militiamen during King Philip's War*, New York: New York University Press, 2010; Richard Henry Marcus, *The Militia of Colonial Connecticut, 1639–1775*, PhD dissertation, Boulder, Colo.: University of Colorado, 1965; John Shy, "Armed Force in Colonial North America: New Spain, New France, and Anglo-America," in Kenneth J. Hagan and William R. Roberts, eds., *Against All Enemies: Interpretations of American Military History from Colonial Times to the Present*, Westport, Conn.: Greenwood Press, 1986; I. F. W. Beckett, *Britain's Part-Time Soldiers: The Amateur Military Tradition 1558–1945*, Barnsley, UK: Pen & Sword Military, 2011; William L. Shea, *The Virginia Militia in the Seventeenth Century*, Baton Rouge, La.: Louisiana State University Press, 1983. The best histories of the American militia are John K. Mahon's numerous articles and books; see John K. Mahon, *The Citizen Soldier in National Defense, 1789–1815*, PhD dissertation, Los Angeles, Calif.: University of California at Los Angeles, 1950; John K. Mahon, "A Board of Officers Considers the Condition of the Militia in 1826," *Military Affairs*, Vol. 15, No. 2, Summer 1951; John K. Mahon, *History of the Second Seminole War, 1835–1842*, Gainesville, Fla.: University Press of Florida, 2010; John K. Mahon, *The American Militia, Decade of Decision, 1789–1800*, Gainesville, Fla.: University Press of Florida, 1960; Mahon, 1983.

community, compared with the death of a land-owning family man. Additionally, this made the drafts less controversial.[3]

As the frontier expanded westward and the colonies grew, the colonial militia systems faced a series of adjustments. For example, a Virginia law passed by the colonial legislature in 1723 for the "better regulation of the militia" gave authority to the chief militia officers throughout the colony to record the names of all white males from ages 21 to 60 "to serve" in militia companies of either "horse or foot."[4] In eastern regions where there was no longer a Native American threat, the compulsory militia units diminished because, without an immediate threat, interest among eastern colonials to regularly muster and train militia companies waned. Colonial British governors insisted, however, that the colonies, through their own expense and training, maintain militia companies in case military force was ever needed. Much like the way the U.S. federal government in the 19th century requested the states to meet certain quotas of militia units for federal service, the British colonial government acted in the same way in the century before the American Revolution. The British frequently cited defense against French aggression as a critical factor for maintaining the compulsory militias, and some colonial militias did indeed combat the French during the French and Indian War (1754–1763) in the northeastern colonies. But even though colonial militias often augmented British forces, the British Army was never impressed by them, both because they lacked the continuous training needed to produce disciplined regular soldiers and because they were unable to serve for extended periods.[5]

Because of the cost of the war, the British government decided to raise revenue by imposing new taxes on the American colonists. From 1761 to 1776, the American colonies staged a series of uprisings and violent protests against British taxation, disturbances suppressed by British Regulars and mercenaries. Exacerbating the growing tension between colonists and the British government was the widespread belief among colonists (rooted in British culture and the civil conflicts of the 17th century) that a standing army in the hands of a monarch was a threat to freedom. Many colonists saw British colonial governors backed by British Army troops as a threat to their liberties.

---

3 See Jason W. Warren, *Connecticut Unscathed: Victory in the Great Narragansett War, 1675–1676*, Norman, Okla.: University of Oklahoma Press, 2014; Harold E. Selesky, *War and Society in Colonial Connecticut,* New Haven, Conn.: Yale University Press, 1990; James David Drake, *King Philip's War: Civil War in New England, 1675–1676*, Amherst, Mass.: University of Massachusetts Press, 1999; Douglas Edward Leach, *Flintlock and Tomahawk: New England in King Philip's War*, New York: MacMillan, 1958.

4 Quoted in Joseph Charles Duggan, *The Legislative and Statutory Development of the Federal Concept of Conscription for Military Service*, Washington, D.C.: Catholic University of America Press, 1946, p. xvii.

5 John Shy, "A New Look at the Colonial Militia," *William and Mary Quarterly*, Vol. 3, No. 20, 1963; Fred Anderson, *A People's Army: Massachusetts Soldiers and Society in the Seven Years' War*, Chapel Hill, N.C.: University of North Carolina Press, 1984; Fred Anderson, *Crucible of War: The Seven Years' War and the Fate of Empire in British North America, 1754–1766*, New York: Alfred A. Knopf, 2000.

During the American Revolution, militia units drawn from the colonies operated together with the nascent American Regular Army, then known as the Continental Army. Individual states used their ability to draft men not only into militia units called for by the Continental Congress but also to meet quotas from Congress to fill the ranks of the Continental Army. In November 1776, the Massachusetts legislature passed a law stipulating that one-quarter of all men on the militia rolls were liable to be drafted into immediate three-month service with the Continental Army. To fill the quota, the state legislature gave local jurisdictions throughout the state the authority to have their militia captains draft men into the Continental line. Militia Captain Samuel Clark of the town of Chelsea, for example, sent a letter to John Sail informing him that:

> . . . you are this evening drafted as one of the Continental men to go to General Washington's headquarters, and you must go or find an able bodied man in your room, or pay a fine of twenty pounds in law, money in twenty-four hours.[6]

Similarly, Pennsylvania's 1776 Constitution made clear that any man enjoying the liberties associated with life in what was once a Quaker homeland owed the larger community his military service, when required.[7] According to Article VIII,

> [E]very member of society hath a right to be protected in the enjoyment of life, liberty and property, and therefore is bound to contribute his proportion towards the expense of that protection, and yield his personal service when necessary, or an equivalent thereto . . . [8]

It is important to note about armies in the political culture of the American colonies and nascent Republic that the colonies/states were the presumed loci of military force: They could and would raise and sustain militias, by means of conscription if they chose. The ways in which each of the thirteen colonies raised militia units varied greatly and depended on the different cultures and laws of each colony, but, in all of them, it was the local community that authorized an appointed militia captain who, when directed, could muster his company and, if needed, compel men into militia service.

Much less certain and far more controversial was the idea that the federal government should also have the ability to raise and maintain armed forces by having some amount of centralized control over the militias of the several states or, beyond that, an

---

6 Quoted in Jonathan Smith, "How Massachusetts Raised Her Troops in the American Revolution," paper presented at Massachusetts Historical Society, January 1922 Meeting: The Plimpton Press, 1922.

7 Pennsylvania's original 1682 "Frame of Government," drafted by the English Quaker leader William Penn, makes no mention of arms or armed forces. Indeed, Pennsylvania until 1776 stood out as the only colony that did not have a militia system, owing no doubt to its Quaker origins.

8 Quoted in M. Farrand, "The Delaware Bill of Rights of 1776," *The American Historical Review*, Vol. 3, 1898, p. 644.

ability to subordinate state forces. Thus, even as late as the 1781 Articles of Confederation, the Continental Congress had no authority to draft men for either militia or Continental Army service, and any new laws that might have provided such authority required the approval of nine of the thirteen proto-states.

Before any debates over military policy could be settled, however, the war for independence had to be won, and state militias would have to help win it. The performance of the militias varied widely depending on the length of service, leadership, and amount of time spent on training. Some militias were better than others, and militias often released militiamen from service soon after summoning them. Responsibility for more than one defeat was laid at the feet of militias who broke ranks and ran in the face of British Regulars, although on other occasions they proved their worth. For example, New York and Vermont militias, combined with Continental Regulars, defeated General John Burgoyne at Saratoga, and the militias at the Battle of Bennington defeated a detachment from Burgoyne's army sent into Vermont to acquire supplies. Probably the best-known victory attributed in part to militias was the Battle of Cowpens in South Carolina in 1781. There, the American commander General Daniel Morgan placed 300 North and South Carolina militiamen in a skirmish line about 300 meters in front of the main battle line of Continental troops. Morgan's orders were for the militiamen to fire only a few volleys at the advancing British, then withdraw behind the Continentals. This worked brilliantly because it capitalized on the strengths of each component. An entire British regiment of nearly 900 soldiers was either killed or captured.[9]

George Washington's "Sentiments on a Peace Establishment"

Victory over Britain did not spell the end of the British threat: Britain retained Canada and had a strong presence in what was then the West, beyond the Appalachian Mountains, where it allied with a number of Native American tribes. France and Spain, moreover, remained well positioned to impose their will on the infant Republic. In addition, there was the threat from Native Americans, not to mention the potential for civil disorder and rebellion. The question was, what should the country do about these threats?

Reflecting on their wartime experience, former Continental Army leaders such as Alexander Hamilton, Henry Knox, Friedrich Wilhelm von Steuben, and George Washington circulated written proposals laying out their ideas about the kind of army the young nation would need in the years ahead. They understood that a large, European-style standing army was unaffordable and unpopular, and therefore out of the question, and they were searching for an adequate alternative.

---

9 Lawrence E. Babits, *A Devil of a Whipping: The Battle of Cowpens*, Chapel Hill, N.C.: University of North Carolina Press, 1998; Burke Davis, *The Cowpens-Guilford Courthouse Campaign*, Philadelphia, Pa.: University of Pennsylvania Press, 2002.

The best known of these pamphlets on the nascent nation's defense posture was Washington's 1783 "Sentiments on a Peace Establishment."[10] Washington acknowledged the sensitivities of his countrymen regarding standing armies—"a large standing army in time of Peace hath ever been considered dangerous to the liberties of a Country"—yet insisted that a small force should be safe.[11] He similarly recognized that, thanks in large part to the Atlantic Ocean, the nation really did not need a large standing force. If circumstances were to change and the country faced a significant threat, it would almost certainly have the time to mobilize an appropriately sized force. Nevertheless, Washington insisted that "a few Troops, under certain circumstances are not only safe, but indispensably necessary."

Washington called for a force of "Continental Troops" made up of 2,631 officers and men. About three-quarters of this force would be in infantry regiments, with a smaller number in artillery, engineer, and cavalry units. Washington believed that the infantry regiments should be intentionally undermanned with privates, but maintained with a full complement of officers. His rationale was to leave room for expanding the infantry units by adding 18 additional private soldiers through increased federal recruitment to each of the eight infantry companies in each regiment. Washington assumed that filling out the ranks of a unit that already had a skeleton of officers would be relatively easy:

> It may also be observed, that in case of War and a necessity of assembling the regiments in the field, nothing more will be necessary, than to recruit 18 men to each company and give the regiment its flank company.[12]

Washington thought differently of artillery, engineer, and cavalry units because they required greater skill and more equipment. Washington did not think they could be expanded quickly and instead called for manning them at nearly 100 percent in peacetime.[13] Washington also understood that the kinds of skills required of artillery and engineers had to be cultivated, and he consequently argued for creating a military academy that would develop the art of war and provide the Continental Troops with professional officers.[14]

---

10 George Washington, "Sentiments on a Peace Establishment" (May 2, 1783), in John C. Fitzpatrick, ed., *The Writings of George Washington from the Original Manuscript Sources, 1745–1799*, Vol. 26, Washington, D.C.: U.S. Government Printing Office, 1938.

11 Washington, 1938, p. 380.

12 Washington, 1938, p. 380.

13 Washington, 1938, pp. 381, 397.

14 Washington believed that an American military academy was both essential and urgent. Without it, the young nation might forget the hard-fought martial knowledge gained during the Revolutionary War and be forced once again to rely upon foreign advisory efforts in future conflicts. He suggested a curriculum of engineering and artillery skills for young officers because "this species of knowledge will render them much more accom-

Washington understood that the small size of the Continental Army meant that the nation would have to rely on local militias; there was no alternative. Washington hoped, however, that the states could maintain their militias at higher levels of readiness and general competency than what he had known to date. The basic idea was to "regulate" the militias and impose rules that ensured a modicum of quality, consistency, and interoperability with each other and with the standing Regular Army. More specifically, Washington called for all (white) American males between the ages of 18 and 50 to be entered into the state militia rolls, an idea that, as we have seen, was familiar to Americans. From the militia rolls, Washington wanted a select portion mustered regularly during the year, including a five-day annual encampment. These men would be younger—between the ages of 18 and 25—and would serve as a "continental militia" or "national militia" that, owing to its relatively high state of readiness, could be called upon more quickly than the rest of the militias to serve alongside the Regulars.[15] Although Washington saw this select militia being formed by states in respective regiments, he also apparently believed it could be used as source of manpower to fill out the ranks of understrength Regular regiments. Washington referred to the remainder of the men in the state militias as "reserved for some great occasion," a national emergency such as a large insurrection or invasion by a foreign army.[16]

Washington wanted this select national militia to train 15 to 25 days per year. The training would be divided between individual soldier instruction and company, battalion, and regimental training. Nonetheless he rejected the national militia having artillery and engineering outfits, for he reckoned even 25 days to be inadequate to obtain any real proficiency. As Washington noted,

> [A] *corps* of able engineers or expert artillerists cannot be raised in a day, nor made such by any exertions, in the same time, which it would take to form an excellent body of infantry from a well-regulated militia.[17]

Notwithstanding Washington's influence, Congress in the years between the end of the Revolution and 1789, when the Constitution went into effect, made no moves in favor of a national military. The Continental Army effectively dissolved, leaving the states to maintain or neglect their militias, as they saw fit. Nonetheless, Washington's work could be seen as an opening salvo in the military policy debate that emerged amid the discussions that brought about the Constitution.

---

plished and capable of performing" any duties required, "even in the infantry or any other Corps whatsoever" (Washington, 1938, pp. 396–397).

[15] Washington, 1938, p. 389.

[16] Washington, 1938, p. 390.

[17] Washington, 1938, p. 397.

Framing the U.S. Constitution

At the end of the 1780s and into the 1790s, the United States faced three security challenges. The first was the threat represented by European nations—above all Great Britain, but also increasingly France. Although this threat was mostly naval, the possibility of invasions or raids on American territory was real. The second challenge was internal. Shays' Rebellion (1786–1787) and the Whiskey Rebellion (1791–1794) were symptomatic of the need to have a military establishment that could help, as the U.S. Constitution would stipulate, to "execute the Laws of the Union [and] suppress Insurrections."[18] The third challenge was the shifting and growing western frontier and the associated conflicts with Native Americans.

The leaders of the early Republic, foremost among them the representatives in the Constitutional Convention (the "Framers"), shared an antipathy toward the idea of having a large standing army and favored relying on organized militias. They were divided, however, on whether there should be a standing Regular force at all and, if so, what its role should be; on the nature of the militias; and on their relationship with federal and state authorities. As we have seen, those who favored a strong, centralized federal government (Hamilton, Knox, Washington, et al.), and came to be known as Federalists, tended to favor a small standing army that would expand when needed, by drawing either individual soldiers or whole units from the states' militias into federal control. Generally in line with Washington's 1783 "Sentiments on a Peace Establishment," they suggested that there were distinct qualitative differences between a Regular Army force and a militia force, and that the garrisoning of frontier posts necessitated a standing force rather than a rotating militia force. They also argued that a standing army was more of a deterrent to European powers than a land defense based solely on the states' militias.[19] That said, they felt it important to place a significant share of the nation's security on the shoulders of militias, which, among other things, could assuage the fears of some by posing as a counter to the perceived potential threat of a standing force, as well as avoid much of the expense associated with a standing force.

For example, James Madison in *The Federalist Papers* (No. 46) argued in favor of a standing regular army: "Let a regular army, fully equal to the resources of the country,

---

[18] Upton, 1903. Commonly referred to as the First Militia Clause, the full sentence empowers Congress "To provide for calling forth the Militia to execute the Laws of the Union, suppress Insurrections and repel Invasions." It was not just British raids that were of concern. Hamilton and other Federalists thought that there was a possibility of a war with France as a consequence of the French Revolution. See Stephen G. Kurtz, "The French Mission of 1799–1800: Concluding Chapter in the Statecraft of John Adams," *Political Science Quarterly*, Vol. 80, No. 4, 1965.

[19] Richard H. Kohn, *Eagle and Sword: Federalists and the Creation of the Military Establishment in America, 1783–1802*, New York: Free Press, 1975; Michael J. Malbin, "Conscription, the Constitution, and the Framers: A Historical Analysis," *Fordham Law Review*, Vol. 40, May 1972; Leon Friedman, "Conscription and the Constitution: The Original Understanding," *Michigan Law Review*, Vol. 67, May 1969.

be formed, and let it be entirely at the devotion of the federal government."[20] However, he hastened to explain that it would pose no threat to liberty given its probable size relative to the size of the militia and people's far greater devotion to the state governments that controlled them. The army, he reasoned, probably would be no larger than "twenty-five or thirty thousand men." In contrast, the states would wield militias that, when combined, would amount "to near half a million of citizens with arms in their hands, officered by men chosen from among them, fighting for their common liberties, and united and conducted by governments possessing their affections and confidence." Besides, Madison added, the course of the War of Independence proved that it would take a very large regular army indeed to suppress the United States. "Those who are best acquainted with the last successful resistance of this country against the British arms will be most inclined to deny the possibility of it," Madison insisted.[21]

In contrast, critics of a standing army, who also tended to be critical of the Constitution and the idea of erecting a strong federal government, emphasized the danger posed by standing armies and the belief that the states needed their own military counterbalance to the powers of the federal government. America's earliest negative experiences with a standing army had been with the British Army in the years leading up to the American Revolution. Americans perceived the British Army to be separated from the society it served and to be more a tool for suppressing internal dissent than for providing security against external threats. The militia advocates wanted an army drawn from, and representative of, their society. They believed that the universal personal obligation of being a member of the militia created that connection. They thought,

---

[20] Alexander Hamilton, James Madison, John Jay, and Lawrence Goldman, eds., *The Federalist Papers*, New York: Oxford University Press, 2008, p. 237.

[21] In *The Federalist Papers* (No. 29), Hamilton advocated for an appropriately sized, well-regulated, and trained militia similar to an organized military. Were the militia to be too large, attempting to train and discipline "all the militia of the United States" would be

> as futile as it would be injurious, if it were capable of being carried into execution. A tolerable expertness in military movements is a business that requires time and practice. It is not a day, or even a week, that will suffice for the attainment of it. To oblige the great body of the yeomanry, and of the other classes of the citizens, to be under arms for the purpose of going through military exercises and evolutions, as often as might be necessary to acquire the degree of perfection which would entitle them to the character of a well-regulated militia, would be a real grievance to the people, and a serious public inconvenience and loss. (Hamilton et al., 2008, p. 237)

Hamilton argued that requiring citizens to train for a considerable amount of time each year rather than work would have economic ramifications:

> To attempt a thing which would abridge the mass of labor and industry to so considerable an extent, would be unwise: and the experiment, if made, could not succeed, because it would not long be endured. Little more can reasonably be aimed at, with respect to the people at large, than to have them properly armed and equipped; and in order to see that this be not neglected, it will be necessary to assemble them once or twice in the course of a year. (Hamilton et al., 2008, p. 140)

moreover, that the diffusion of military power—making the federal government reliant on the states to raise the army—was an important check on federal power.[22]

A good example of this type of criticism can be found in the letters from the anonymous "Federalist Farmer" to "the Republican" (1788):

> The military forces of a free country may be considered under three general descriptions — 1. The militia. 2. The navy — and 3. the regular troops — and the whole ought ever to be, and understood to be, in strict subordination to the civil authority; and that regular troops, and select corps, ought not to be kept up without evident necessity. Stipulations in the constitution to this effect, are perhaps, too general to be of much service, except merely to impress on the minds of the people and soldiery, that the military ought ever to be subject to the civil authority, &c. But particular attention, and many more definite stipulations, are highly necessary to render the military safe, and yet useful in a free government; and in a federal republic, where the people meet in distinct assemblies, many stipulations are necessary to keep a part from transgressing, which would be unnecessary checks against the whole met in one legislature, in one entire government. — A militia, when properly formed, are in fact the people themselves, and render regular troops in a great measure unnecessary.[23]

The Federalist Farmer acknowledged that all nations needed to be able to raise regular troops, but he rejected the need for a peacetime force and was above all concerned that the federal government's capacity to raise or control forces of any kind be hemmed in by laws that divided it among branches of the federal government and limited it vis-à-vis the states. There should never be a peacetime army; the federal government should raise an army only when absolutely necessary; it should be able to do so only with the full support of Congress; and that army should have a fixed and short expiration date. The anonymous writer went so far as to express discomfort with having a "select" federal militia, that is, units kept at high states of readiness and under federal control, for fear that it would amount to the same thing as a regular force and also cause governments to neglect the standard militias:

> . . . [T]he constitution ought to secure a genuine and guard against a select militia, by providing that the militia shall always be kept well organized, armed, and disciplined, and include, according to the past and general usage of the states, all men

22 For a recently published excellent revisionist history of the ratification debates and debates over the Constitution itself, see Pauline Maier, *Ratification: The People Debate the Constitution, 1787–1788*, New York: Simon & Schuster, 2010. Maier makes a persuasive case that it is incorrect to refer to critics of a standing army and the larger Constitution as Anti-Federalists, since, as she argues, none of them referred to themselves as such, and many of them were actually in favor of some kind of federalist system—they just did not agree with the way the Constitution put it into place.

23 Anonymous, "The Federalist Farmer No. XVIII" (1788), in Herbert J. Storing, ed., *The Complete Anti-Federalist*, Chicago, Ill.: University of Chicago Press, 1981, p. 341.

> capable of bearing arms; and that all regulations tending to render this general militia useless and defenseless, by establishing select corps of militia, or distinct bodies of military men, not having permanent interests and attachments in the community to be avoided.[24]

The key to defending the country in the eyes of the critics was to ensure that everyone (i.e., all white males of a certain age) be organized into local militias that were uniformly but not particularly well trained, given that, as the Federalist Farmer noted, keeping all militias at a high state of drill was neither possible nor a good idea. During the Constitutional Convention, Elbridge Gerry of New York made clear to his fellow participants that giving Congress the power to provide for the "discipline" and to regulate the militia was a direct assault on the liberties of the several states. Gerry argued that giving the federal government that kind of power, even though it rested with Congress and not the President, might very well ". . . enslave the states. Such idea as this will never be acceded to."[25]

What happened during the Constitutional Convention, which opened in 1787, represents more or less a victory for the Framers who desired a strong federal government and their ideas of the proper military establishment for the United States. The Constitution contains five passages that deal directly with the potential for building an army to defend the United States from external invasion and protect against internal rebellion.

The first three passages are in Article I, Section 8. The first of these is known as the "armies clause" and gives Congress the power

> to raise and support Armies, but no Appropriation of Money to that Use shall be for a longer Term than two Years; To provide and maintain a Navy.

The second passage is known as the "calling forth clause" and allows Congress

> to provide for calling forth the Militia to execute the Laws of the Union, suppress Insurrections and repel Invasions . . .

The third passage is known more simply as the "militia clause" and allows Congress

> to provide for organizing, arming, and disciplining, the Militia, and for governing such Part of them as may be employed in the Service of the United States, reserving to the States respectively, the Appointment of the Officers, and the Authority of training the militia according to the discipline prescribed by Congress.

---

24 Anonymous, 1981, p. 341.

25 *The Papers of James Madison, Purchased by Order of Congress; Being His Correspondence and Reports of Debates During the Congress of the Confederation and His Reports of Debates in the Federal Convention*, Vol. II, New York: J. & H. G. Langley, 1841, p. 823.

The fourth passage is in Article II, Section 2, and is known as the "Commander in Chief clause." It names the President as

> Commander in Chief of the Army and the Navy of the United States, and of the Militia of the several States, when called into the actual Service of the United States.

The fifth passage is in Article IV, Section 4, and is known as the "guarantee clause":

> The United States shall guarantee to every State in this Union a Republican Form of Government, and shall protect each of them against Invasion; and on the Application of the Legislature, or the Executive (when the Legislature cannot be convened) against domestic violence.

These five passages enshrined within U.S. law the existence of two sources for building an army and enlarging it when needed: a standing (Regular) Army that Congress could "raise and support," and a militia—or more precisely the militias—of the several states. The states would form their militias, appoint their officers, and train them, but Congress would be able to impose its discipline and will when it called the militias to federal duty in the "service of the United States." Thus, the Constitution places the Regular Army, and the nationalized militias when federalized, under the President's command, but grants Congress the power to raise and sustain the Army and mandates a time limit on appropriations. Of note is the care with which the Constitution divides power between the President and Congress, on one hand, and the federal government and the states, on the other. One might go so far as to argue that the Framers were more concerned with balancing these powers than they were with endowing the Republic with adequate military strength.

As for the militias, the two militia clauses divided power between the federal government and the states. Congress could call forth and provide for state militias, but the Constitution nonetheless stipulated that the states would remain in control of the training and the appointment of officers when not in federal service, which maintained the connection between the militias and state governors and presumably a degree of loyalty. The states, it should be remembered, were expected to have some military capability. Or at least the idea of states maintaining militaries seemed more normal in late 18th century American political culture than the idea of a standing federal force. Pennsylvania's 1790 Constitution, for example, appears to take for granted the idea that Pennsylvania should have an army and a navy, with the governor commanding both, provided, of course, that a standing army in peacetime have the consent of the Pennsylvania legislature (Article IX, Section XXII). As for the militia, all "freemen of this commonwealth shall be armed and disciplined for its defence" (Article VI, Section II). In other words, Pennsylvania could compel military service, yet there was no comparable law enabling the federal government to conscript soldiers.

In the initial division of roles envisioned by the Framers, the small standing army, which would soon be defined in statutory law as the Regular Army, would be responsible for manning a series of forts in the west and coastal defenses in the east, and for providing a minimal capability to conduct other missions.[26] As we shall see, while the Regular Army would grow in size for the four major wars the United States fought in the 19th century, the Army's fundamental mission did not change, with the result that the logic behind where the troops were stationed remained more or less constant. The Regulars were placed where a "first line of defense" would most likely be needed, and where armed force was a likely requirement even in peacetime. Moreover, although the Framers understood that the Regular Army would be used in the event of a general war, they realized that they could not afford to build and sustain a standing army large enough to fight a war against a major power. Nor did the Framers expect the standing army to be able to enter into such a fight alone or quickly. In peacetime, Regulars served as coastal defense and along the frontier to deal with Native American challenges to westward expansion, and also provided domestic support in areas such as exploration and civil works.[27]

To fight large-scale wars, the Constitution empowered Congress to "raise" an army. However, the Constitution did not detail how this should be done, and several opinions existed. Some felt that Congress could directly recruit individuals into the Regular Army. Others argued that Congress could only muster militia members, militia units, and federal volunteers into service. Finally, some felt that the Army could be based solely on the militias by leveraging the states—when needed, the state militias would provide volunteers, who would be equipped and organized into Army units by their given state.

Following the constitutional debates, the Framers issued a series of amendments intended to strengthen the balance of power between the state and federal governments and guarantee individual liberty.[28]

---

26 Kohn, 1975, pp. 42–44.

27 Edward M. Coffman, *The Old Army: A Portrait of the American Army in Peacetime, 1784–1898*, New York: Oxford University Press, 1986, pp. 3–6.

28 For scholarship specifically on the Second Amendment, see Weigley, 1984, p. 87; John Kenneth Rowland, *Origins of the Second Amendment: The Creation of the Constitutional Rights of Militia and of Keeping and Bearing Arms*, PhD dissertation, Columbus, Ohio: Ohio State University, 1978; Saul Cornell, *A Well-Regulated Militia: The Founding Fathers,and the Origins of the Gun Control Debate in America*, New York: Oxford University Press, 2006, pp. 11–13; Charles A. Lofgren, "Compulsory Service Under the Constitution: The Original Understanding," *The William and Mary Quarterly*, Vol. 33, No. 1, January 1976, pp. 61–88; Lawrence Delbert Cress, "A Well-Regulated Militia: The Origins and Meaning of the Second Amendment," in Saul Cornell, ed., *Whose Right to Bear Arms Did the Second Amendment Protect?* Boston, Mass.: Bedford/St. Martin's, 2000.

Conclusion

By way of summary, we should emphasize that no one involved in the writing or ratification of the Constitution argued for a large standing force. Nevertheless, the Federalists focused on ensuring the professional qualities of the Regular Army, however small, and doing what they could to endow the militias with comparable virtues. They did not want to rely on amateur civilian-soldiers. Others viewed the militias as the heart of the military establishment and placed great stock in the citizenry's ability to rise to the occasion to defend the nation.[29] In the end, the Federalist framers got what they wanted: license to build a federal standing army and exercise some federal control over the militia. It was up to successive governments to fill in many of the remaining details, work out precisely how much of a standing army the country needed, and determine the relationship between the federal government and the militias of the several states. In most instances, implementation would fall far short of the Federalists' ambitions, largely because of the strength of the inherited antipathy toward standing armies, a political culture that associated local militias with democracy and republican virtue, and the absence of fiscal resources to do otherwise. Military policy after the Constitution was invariably a compromise between these two sides and their heirs.

---

[29] See Maier, 2010; Anonymous, 1981; David P. Currie, *The Constitution in Congress: The Federalist Period 1789–1801*, Chicago, Ill.: University of Chicago Press, 1997; Jack N. Rakove, *Original Meanings: Politics and Ideas in the Making of the Constitution*, New York: A. A. Knopf, 1996; Willi Paul Adams, *The First American Constitutions: Republican Ideology and the Making of the State Constitutions in the Revolutionary Era*, Chapel Hill, N.C.: Published for the Institute of Early American History and Culture, Williamsburg, Virginia, by the University of North Carolina Press, 1980.

CHAPTER THREE

Adapting the Constitution to the Security Demands of the New Republic

Introduction

Initially, the Republic struggled to maintain even the smallest Regular Army and could barely cope with threats posed by Native Americans and internal rebellions, let alone the risk of invasion by foreign powers. The Regular Army had a meager strength of 800 soldiers and relied on local militias produced by the states to expand when needed. However, both the Regular Army and the militias were critically under-resourced, resulting in a force incapable of conducting effective operations on the frontier. This point was brought home in 1791 when Native American tribes decisively defeated a combined force of 350 Regular Army troops and 1,100 militiamen during a series of deadly engagements known as St. Clair's Defeat, or the Battle of the Wabash, in the Northwestern Territory of Ohio. In the last of these deadly clashes, a detachment of approximately 60 Regulars and 300 militiamen were cut off from the larger force and attacked, causing the majority of the militiamen to flee and leading to the virtual annihilation of the remaining Regular troops.[1]

The Constitution and its first ten amendments certainly established the framework for the nation to have both a Regular Army and state militias that might be used in some way to increase the size of the Army when needed. However, the way in which Congress might actually go about "organizing, arming, and disciplining" the militias, as the militia clause stipulated, would need to be hammered out in statutory law. Shortly after assuming office as the first President of the United States, George Washington pushed Congress to enact a law that would establish what he called in his 1783 "Sentiments" a "well-regulated militia." Indeed, Washington had his Secretary of War and former subordinate during the American Revolution, Henry Knox, draw up a plan for providing federal oversight of the militias of the several states in what both of them hoped would be a newly passed law. In 1792, Congress did pass a law on the militia; however, as the following sections will show, it did not come anywhere close to the kind of system Washington and Knox had envisioned. Instead, the Uniform Mili-

1 Kohn, 1975, pp. 115–116.

tia Act of 1792 was a watered-down law that stipulated how the state militias should be organized, trained, and equipped but failed to provide any mechanism to ensure compliance by the states.[2] The law also failed to establish how the state militias would expand the size of the Army when needed.

At the same time that Congress passed its first militia bill, it was also experiencing a demand that the Constitution did not really anticipate: the need for the President to be able to "call forth" the militias of the several states to deal with significant internal unrest that state and local magistrates could not handle. Whereas the Constitution allowed Congress only to "call forth" the militia to deal with lawlessness, insurrection, and invasion, the first handful of years for the early Republic showed the need for a more central authority—namely, the President—to respond quickly to such unrests. As a result, Congress passed three important laws between 1792 and 1807 that greatly increased the power of the President to call forth the militia and even use the Regular forces to deal with internal unrest. These three laws, as we explain below, moved significantly away from the Constitution's notion of the militias, the Regular Army, and presidential authority in dealing with internal unrest.

The Uniform Militia Act of 1792

The Constitution's provision of a means to raise military forces came not a moment too soon, given the young Republic's struggle to contend with mounting violence on its frontier. Already, in 1789, the new American government had committed itself to rebuilding the nation's forces from virtually nothing to a small Regular Army consisting of an eight-company regiment of infantry and a four-company battalion of artillery.[3] This raised the overall authorized strength of the Regular Army to 840 men, although by 1789 only a paltry 672 men filled its ranks.[4] Native Americans decisively defeated the Army in 1790, prompting Congress in 1791 to increase the size of the authorized force. St. Clair's Defeat in 1791 at the hands of Native Americans prompted Congress to raise its commitment in 1792, this time to five regiments of infantry with cavalry and artillery support, roughly 5,000 men. General Anthony Wayne led this force to victory at the battle of Fallen Timbers in 1794.[5]

---

2 U.S. Statutes at Large, An Act to More Effectually to Provide for the National Defense by Establishing a Uniform Militia Throughout the United States, 1792.

3 U.S. Statutes at Large, An Act to Recognize and Adapt to the Constitution of the United States, the Establishment of the Troops Raised Under the Resolve of the United States in Congress Assembled and for Other Purposes Therein Mentioned, First Congress, Sessions I and II, Chapter 25, September 29, 1789.

4 Russell Frank Weigley, *History of the United States Army*, Bloomington, Ind.: Indiana University Press, 1984, p. 89.

5 James Ripley Jacobs, *The Beginning of the U.S. Army, 1783–1812*, Princeton, N.J.: Princeton University Press, 1947; Richard G. Stone, *A Brittle Sword: The Kentucky Militia, 1776–1912*, Lexington, Ky.: University Press of

In 1792, President Washington and his advisers, foremost among them Secretary of War Knox, pushed for legislation they hoped would strengthen the nation's defense by placing on a firm footing through federal regulation and oversight the militias of the several states that could be drawn into federal service when needed to increase the size of the Army. They hoped to establish a "well-regulated" militia, with Knox promoting a plan that drew on previous proposals by Washington, Hamilton, and von Steuben.[6]

Knox called for tiered militias, with some tiers trained to a higher standard than others. Under Knox's plan, the militias would be armed and equipped at the expense of the federal government, whereas previously it had been solely up to the militiamen themselves or the states to fund and maintain their militias.[7] Young recruits aged 18 and 19 would train for 30 days each year, while 20-year-olds would train 10 days per year. Equally important in Knox's plan was the idea that every white American male between the ages of 18 and 45 (after age 45, they would become part of the "Reserved Corps") owed military duty to the nation through service in the militias. This 18–45 age range had generally been codified in local and colonial laws prior to the Revolution.[8] Knox thought the militias would work best if accompanied by institutions "for the military education of youth" and for the diffusion of military education "throughout the community by the principles of rotation."[9]

The bill that passed, which became known as the Uniform Militia Act of 1792, provided guidance to the states for them to discipline and organize their militias. It stipulated such things as a standardized organizational construct, the types of equipment that the militia should maintain, and militia chains of command, to include state Adjutants General.

However, the act turned out to be substantially weaker than Knox had wanted, and was tantamount to a step backward. As historian Richard Kohn has remarked:

> The calls for reform which began in 1783 and culminated in the act of 1792 revealed that many Americans sensed the inability of state institutions, poorly coordinated,

---

Kentucky, 2009; Mahon, 1950; Allan D. Gaff, *Bayonets in the Wilderness: Anthony Wayne's Legion in the Old Northwest*, Norman, Okla.: University of Oklahoma Press, 2004.

6 Russell Frank Weigley, *Towards an American Army: Military Thought from Washington to Marshall*, New York: Columbia University Press, 1962.

7 John O'Sullivan and Alan M. Meckler, *The Draft and Its Enemies: A Documentary History*, Champaign, Ill.: University of Illinois Press, 1974, pp. 28–36; Kohn, 1975, pp. 128–138; Henry Knox, *A Plan for the General Arrangement of the Militia of the United States*, New York: Francis Childs and John Swaine, 1790; Richard H. Kohn, "The Murder of the Militia System in the Aftermath of the American Revolution," in Stanley J. Underdal, ed., *Military History of the American Revolution: The Proceedings of the 6th Military History Symposium of the United States Air Force Academy 10–11 October 1974*, Washington, D.C.: U.S. Government Printing Office, 1976; Weigley, 1962.

8 U.S. Statutes at Large, An Act to More Effectually to Provide for the National Defense by Establishing a Uniform Militia Throughout the United States, 1792.

9 Knox, 1790, p. 7.

> badly disciplined, and casually armed to meet the needs of the New Republic. . . . The act looked backward to colonial times, to a simpler military environment, to localism in defense when citizens could provide security by defending themselves. . . .[10]

The act created no enforcement mechanisms to ensure that the states would comply with its stipulations on raising, training, and supplying the militia units; the law was more aspirational than legally binding on the states. In the years ahead, therefore, only a few militia companies became respectable military units of the sort that Knox desired; whether they did so—and whether and how the act was enforced at all—depended on the vagaries and interests of the various states toward their militias. Most states prescribed fines and imprisonment for those who refused service, and relied on regional enforcement. Some states allowed for exemptions from militia service: For example, in recognition of the importance of public safety, the state of New York exempted all firemen from militia service, due to their localized importance during times of peace and war. The Uniform Militia Act also exempted certain individuals from militia service, such as the Vice President of the United States, "post officers and stage drivers," and members of both houses of Congress, among others.

The 1792 Uniform Militia Act had another significant shortcoming, which would take nearly another century to rectify: It did not link the militias to the Regular Army or otherwise establish their relationship with the Regular Army. Certainly, the Constitution provided a theoretical linkage between the two, but it did not specify how in practice to forge that linkage. The 1792 Uniform Militia Act did not define the militias of the several states as reserve forces for the Army. What developed instead during the 19th century was an informal method for expanding the size of the Army in times of war through multiple parallel mechanisms, with the states and the federal government alike calling for volunteers, and the states supplying both volunteers and compulsory militiamen.[11]

The 1792 Uniform Militia Act contains other noteworthy elements. First, it used the word *called* when referring to the militia, a reference to the first militia clause of the Constitution.[12] Although the term was not exceptional by 1792, as the 19th century progressed and the armies clause became increasingly important for expanding

---

10 Kohn, 1975, p. 137.

11 Marcus Cunliffe, *Soldiers and Civilians: The Martial Spirit in America, 1775–1865*, Boston, Mass.: Little, Brown, 1968; Walter Millis, *American Military Thought*, Indianapolis, Ind.: Bobbs-Merrill, 1966; Emory Upton, *The Military Policy of the United States*, 4th ed., Washington, D.C.: U.S. Government Printing Office, 1903; Russell Frank Weigley, *History of the United States Army*, New York: Macmillan, 1967; Ricardo A. Herrera, *For Liberty and the Republic: The American Citizen as Soldier, 1775–1861*, New York: New York University Press, 2015; Kohn, 1975.

12 For the best treatment of the 1792 Uniform Militia Act, see John K. Mahon, *The American Militia: Decade of Decision, 1789–1800*, 1960.

the Army, a new term, *ordered,* began to be used instead of *called,* showing a different constitutional premise for expanding the Army. Second, the Uniform Militia Act stipulated the enrollment of "every able-bodied white male citizen" between 18 and 45 and the organization of the militia into divisions, brigades, regiments, battalions, and companies by the individual states, with each militiaman providing his own "arms, munitions, and other accouterments."[13] In this sense, it designated a form of universal (for white males) military obligation and relied on state militia captains to "enroll" the eligible population within their geographic areas. This established the basis for conscription into state and federal service throughout the 19th century.

Congressional debates over the Uniform Militia Act provide insights into why the final act was very different from what Washington and Knox had envisioned and proposed. One of the central points of contention, as it was during the Constitutional Convention debates, was where power should lie with regard both to organizing, equipping, and training the state militias and to the authority to call them forth. Representative Jonathan Sturges of Connecticut reportedly argued that the power to train, equip, and determine exemptions from militia service rested with the states and that Congress should have the authority to "organize" the militias only when they were first called forward for service. In response, another congressman, clearly of the Federalist persuasion, noted that the "consequence" of Sturges's "motion would be, to render the power of Congress in organizing, arming and disciplining the militia, entirely nugatory."[14] Although Federalist arguments like these were made, it was clear that the majority of Congress favored a defanged version of the Knox bill, which ultimately came to be the final act. Representative Abraham Clark of New Jersey noted sarcastically that if Congress were given the centralizing authorities over the militia, as the Knox bill proposed, then if "an old woman was to strike an excise officer with a broomstick, forsooth the military is to be called out to suppress an insurgency."[15]

The 1792 Calling Forth Act

At the same time that members of Congress debated the Uniform Militia Act, they also deliberated over what would become known as the Calling Forth Act. With the persistent threat of Native American attacks on the frontier, and with the ever-present possibility of internal insurrections,

---

13 Richard W. Stewart, *American Military History, Volume II: The United States Army in a Global Era, 1917–2008*, Washington, D.C.: U.S. Army Center of Military History, 2010, p. 114.

14 *Congressional Record, Annals of Congress*, 2nd Congress, 1st Session, February 21, 1792, p. 419.

15 *Congressional Record, Annals of Congress*, 2nd Congress, 2nd Session, April 23, 1792, p. 575.

such as Shays' Rebellion, Congress felt the need to provide more authority to the President to respond to such challenges.[16] On May 2, 1792—six days before passage of the Uniform Militia Act—Congress passed the Calling Forth Act.[17] Whereas the Constitution gave *only* Congress the authority to "provide for calling forth the militia," the new law provided the President with the authority to call forth the militia of the several states to suppress insurrections, repel invasions, and enforce the laws of the land. However, Congress placed certain restrictions on the President, including the requirement that he receive an antecedent court order—a judicial certificate—from a local magistrate or state official inviting the President to call forth the militias to deal with problems inside a state or a group of states that local governmental power could not manage.[18] Congress was only seasonally in session during this period, and the judicial certificate created an avenue for the executive powers to utilize the militia while Congress was not in session. In other words, when it came to dealing with internal unrest and enforcing the laws of the land, the President did not enjoy the independent authority to call forth the militias; he could act only in response to a request by local officials. But in a following section of the Calling Forth Act, Congress gave the President unhindered authority to call for the militias of the several states when responding to foreign invasion. As a result, this Calling Forth Act was a significant departure from the militia envisioned by the Constitution, because the Framers' debates showed that Congress, and not the President, was to be the branch of the federal government that would have sole authority for "calling forth the militia."

Unsatisfied by the Calling Forth Act's provisions, some continued to agitate for reform because they perceived the need to vest more authority in the President to respond quickly to internal crises by calling forth the militias himself. In March 1794, Congress debated proposals to authorize the President to raise 10,000 Regular troops and to order the states to organize and hold in readiness the militia. Neither gained

---

16 At its heart, the 1786–1787 rebellion was the result of socioeconomic grievances. A postwar depression made it difficult for farmers—many of whom, including their leader, Daniel Says, were Revolutionary War veterans who had fought without remuneration—to pay off growing debts and high taxes. The roughly organized rebellion swept across central and western Massachusetts as protestors interrupted legal proceedings for tax and debt collection. Tensions peaked on January 25, 1787, when 1,500 farmers attempted to seize arms from the Springfield Armory and met resistance from local militias. The insurrection indicated the young government's inability to suppress domestic disturbances or to address their root causes. See Leonard L. Richards, *Shay's Rebellion: The American Revolution's Final Battle*, Philadelphia, Pa.: University of Pennsylvania Press, 2002; Daniel P. Szatmary, *The Making of an Agrarian Insurrection*, Amherst, Mass.: University of Massachusetts Press, 1980; Robert A. Gross, "A Yankee Rebellion? The Regulators, New England, and the New Nation," *New England Quarterly*, Vol. 82, No. 1, March 2009.

17 U.S. Statutes at Large, An Act Providing for Calling Forth the Militia to Execute the Laws of the Union, Suppress Insurrections, and Repel Invasions, Second Congress, Session I, Chapter 28, May 2, 1792 (1 Stat. 264).

18 See David E. Engdahl, "Soldiers, Riots, and Revolutions: The Law and History of Military Troops in Civil Disorders," *Iowa Law Review*, Vol. 57, No. 1, October 1971; Robert Coakley, *The Role of Federal Military Forces in Domestic Disorders, 1789–1878*, Washington, D.C.: U.S. Army Center of Military History, 1989.

traction. As the young Republic struggled to build a sustainable economy, strengthening the military establishment appeared, as one congressman noted at the time, to be "a very useless expense."[19]

The 1795 Calling Forth Act and the 1807 Insurrection Act

The culmination of the Whiskey Rebellion in July 1794 drew attention back to the problem of the nation's ability to suppress internal rebellion and dissent. On August 7, Washington drew on the 1792 Uniform Militia Act to mobilize 13,000 militiamen to quell the insurgency. The militias performed well below expectations: Incidents of desertion and cowardice were widespread, leading Representative Samuel Smith of Maryland to complain that the militias of the Southern States "were totally useless for the professed purposes of the institution."[20] Congressional concern over the federal government's difficulty in responding to civil unrest, coupled with trust in President Washington and the calm, even-handed manner with which he handled the insurgents, overcame initial fears that strengthening the President's control over the militia might tip the fragile relationship between the federal government and the states.[21] To Representative Theodore Sedgwick of Massachusetts, an active voice for reform, it now appeared "anti-Republican to attempt to narrow the powers of this Government over the militia."[22] In the February 1795 Calling Forth Act, Congress lifted some of

---

19 *Congressional Record, Annals of Congress*, 3rd Congress, 1st Session, May 30, 1794, p. 736. For a detailed analysis of the legal history behind the executive's emergency powers and congressional delegation of that authority to the presidency, see Stephen I. Vladeck, "Emergency Power and the Militia Acts," *The Yale Law Review*, Vol. 114, October 2004.

20 *Congressional Record, Annals of Congress*, 3rd Congress, 2nd Session, February 12, 1795, p. 1214. In March 1791, Congress enacted an excise tax on distilled spirits in order to pay off war debts. As whiskey was the principal product of farmers' harvests on the frontier—large numbers of them Revolutionary War veterans—the tax cut hard into what little profits they could expect for their efforts. Many perceived the tax as unlawful, the act of a tyrannical government meant only to enrich war financiers, and therefore resisted paying. In Western Pennsylvania, confrontations over collectors and protestors escalated and finally compelled President Washington to lead the federalized militia into the area in October 1794. See Terry Bouton, *Taming Democracy: "The People," the Founders, and the Troubled Ending of the American Revolution*, New York: Oxford University Press, 2007; Steven R. Boyd, ed., *The Whiskey Rebellion: Past and Present Perspectives*, Westport, Conn.: Greenwood Press, 1985; Richard H. Kohn, "The Washington Administration's Decision to Crush the Whiskey Rebellion," *Journal of American History*, Vol. 59, No. 3, December, 1972.

21 William L. Shaw, "The Interrelationship of the United States Army and the National Guard," *Military Law Review*, No. 39, January 1966, pp. 47–49; David J. Barron and Martin S. Ledermen, "The Commander in Chief at the Lowest Ebb: A Constitutional History," *Harvard Law Review*, Vol. 1, No. 4, February 2008, pp. 956–957, 961–964; Alan Hirsch, "The Militia Clause of the Constitution and the National Guard," *University of Cincinnati Law Review*, No. 59, 1988, pp. 930–939; Michael Bahar, "The Presidential Intervention Principle: The Domestic Use of the Military and the Power of the Several States," *Harvard National Security Journal*, Vol. 5, 2014, pp. 579–582.

22 *Congressional Record, Annals of Congress*, February 12, 1795, p. 1214.

the 1792 Calling Forth Act's restrictions and authorized the President to directly "call forth" the militias for the purpose of suppressing civil disturbances.[23] This was made possible by the removal of the primary safeguard mandated in the 1792 act, the judicial certificate. By eliminating this, Congress affirmed the President's ability to call forth the militias both in the case of foreign invasion and when domestic matters demanded their use, notwithstanding the Constitution's intent on entrusting that power exclusively with Congress itself.

One of the implications of this change was a shift away from the Constitution's depiction of the use of the militias of the several states and the Regular Army. Many of the Framers envisioned the local militias as the tool of choice for dealing with local civil and domestic matters, and they intended to reserve the Regular Army for service along the frontier and, in concert with mobilized local militias, for repelling an invasion by a major foreign power.[24] Indeed, it was this combination of the Regular Army and the local militias that made up the nation's "first-line defenses," a term that would become popular in the latter part of the 19th century. By 1795, Congress appeared to be losing interest in this distinction, as reflected in the 1792 and 1795 Calling Forth Acts, and indeed in 1799 Congress temporarily authorized President John Adams to use federal regulars whenever he called forth the militias to manage domestic problems and enforce the law. This expansion of presidential authority was made permanent in the Insurrection Act of 1807.[25] That act effectively abandoned the Constitution's delineation of the circumstances in which the state militias or federal Regulars could be used.[26] According to the 1807 law, in the case of insurrection or obstruction of state or federal laws where the President had legal authority to call for the militias, "it shall be lawful" for the President "to employ, for the same purposes, such part of the land or naval force of the United States as shall be judged necessary."[27] Thus the President, not Congress, had the full authority to call not only the militias to deal with internal challenges but the Regular Army and the Navy, as well.

Despite the President's newfound authority to call forth both the state militias and the Regular Army to manage internal instability and repel invasions, Congress still

---

23 U.S. Statutes at Large, An Act Providing for the Authority for Calling Forth the Militia to Execute the Laws of the Union, Suppress Insurrections, and Repel Invasions; and to Repeal the Act Now in Force for Those Purposes, Third Congress, Session II, Chapter 30, February 28, 1795 (1 Stat. 424).

24 Weigley, 1984, pp. 86–89.

25 U.S. Statutes at Large, An Act Authorizing the Employment of the Land and Naval Forces of the United States, in Case of Insurrections, Tenth Congress, Session II, Chapter 39, March 3, 1807 (2 Stat. 443); Robert Coakley, *Federal Use of Militia and the National Guard in Civil Disturbances*, Washington, D.C: Brookings Institution, 1941; Bennett Milton Rich, *The Presidents and Civil Disorder*, Washington, D.C.: Brookings Institution, 1941; Frederick T. Wilson, *Federal Aid in Domestic Disturbances, 1787–1903*, New York: Arno Press, 1969.

26 Vladeck, 2004, pp. 157–161, 162–166.

27 U.S. Statutes at Large, An Act Authorizing the Employment of the Land and Naval Forces of the United States, in Case of Insurrections, 1807.

had not defined a formal, legal relationship between the militias and the Regular Army or a process to expand the Army in time of war or crisis. In other words, there was still no military policy on the books that governed the U.S. Army and established a legal relationship between the state militias and the Regular Army, and how the Army could be expanded for national emergencies and war. More than a century would pass first before policy would come to resemble what we have today, in which these relationships are documented in Title 10 of the U.S. Code.[28]

Conclusion

The years between the ratification of the Constitution in 1788 by all 13 states and the signing of the Insurrection Act in 1807 saw important changes in the way Congress defined the roles of the militias of the several states and the Regular Army in dealing with internal crises. U.S. leaders shifted away from the Constitution's provision that only Congress had the authority to call forth the militia toward a new position that provided the President with that authority. Congress was motivated to carry out this shift by a perceived need to allow a more centralized, responsive authority—the President—to respond to increasing Native American threats on the frontier and internal challenges more quickly and decisively than the collective body of Congress could. Congress also passed the Uniform Militia Act in 1792, which provided guidance to the states on how they should go about organizing, training, equipping, and disciplining their respective militias, but nothing in the law compelled the states to follow this guidance. In the absence of a statutorily defined military policy during the 19th century, the United States continued to rely entirely on the states to organize, train, and discipline their militias, with little or no ability to influence how they did so.

---

28 Title 10 stipulates that the U.S. Army consists of the "Regular Army, the Army National Guard of the United States, the Army National Guard while in the service of the United States, and the Army Reserve." It also states unequivocally that the purpose of the Army's reserve component is to "provide trained units and qualified persons available for active duty in the armed forces, in time of war or national emergency, and at such other times as the national security may require, to fill the needs of the armed forces whenever more units and persons are needed than are in the regular components."

CHAPTER FOUR

Getting By: Increasing the Size of the Army, the War of 1812, the Mexican War, and the U.S. Civil War

Introduction

The United States fought three major wars between 1812 and 1865 while also using military force against Native Americans on the frontier. Throughout, the country relied on the states and territories to generate militias and volunteer forces to expand the Army when required, but to generally retain a very small and affordable Regular Army as the professional core of the Army. For example, the Regular Army comprised just 7,000 men in 1812, and 15,000 at the start of the Civil War in 1861. Each time the nation had to mobilize larger forces, it did so primarily by using the states and territories to generate militias and volunteer forces. The system worked adequately, although not without considerable disorder and inefficiency, owing in large part to the absence of clear policies and rules establishing precisely how the federal and state governments should proceed.

The Types of 19th Century American Militias

In the 19th century, there were three basic types of militia and two additional types of volunteer forces. Because there were many different types of forces that the states and territories could draw on, and because the various types can often appear quite confusing, it is worth taking the time to explain them. There were three main types of 19th century American militias:

1. common or compulsory militias
2. state-formed volunteer militias for federal service (when levied by Congress)
3. state-sanctioned volunteer militias for federal service.

There were also two types of volunteer forces specific to two of the United States' main conflicts of the 19th century:

1. Civil War volunteer regiments, Union Army
2. federal volunteers for the Spanish-American War.

Another important concept to be aware of is the *militia manpower pool.* According to colonial tradition and laws, the 1792 Uniform Militia Act, and the newly formed states' laws that drew on their colonial roots, all able-bodied (white) males from ages 18 to 45 were liable for militia service. In effect, these laws produced a militia manpower pool in that virtually all American white men within a certain age range were in it. As we discuss the five specific types of 19th century American militias and volunteer forces listed above, keep in mind that technically all of them consisted of individual American militiamen from the start, as they were all part of the militia manpower pool, in accordance with federal and state laws and traditions.

Compulsory or Common Militias

Until the War of 1812 (explained in more detail below), the federal government expanded the Army primarily through the calling forth of *common* or *compulsory* militias, in which theoretically all white men of a certain age were enrolled, as per the 1792 Uniform Militia Act (which reaffirmed in federal statute the authority of the states to form compulsory militias and provided guidance to the states for how they should be trained and organized, even though it provided no enforcement mechanisms for the states to do so along federal lines). As a result, each state's constitution outlined an independent process for the organizing, training, and equipping of their common militias, and the ways in which, when called on by the federal government, the state would produce militia units for federal service.

When the federal government needed to use the state militias to increase the size of the Army for federal service, it would send each state a requested quota of militia companies or regiments. That quota would filter its way down to the militia companies, where the officer in charge would direct a gathering of all the men in the company. The quotas were usually for a small portion of the company's overall strength, and the commanding officer would often first ask for volunteers. If he was unable to furnish the requested number of men, he had the authority under state laws (and the 1792 Uniform Militia Act, which compelled all men between the ages of 18 and 45 to militia service) to draft militia members into active service. Once a sufficient number of men were designated, they would then join a new company organized as a composite of multiple town militias that were selected in the same way.[1]

---

[1] William D. Pratt, *A History of the National Guard of Indiana: From the Beginning of the Militia System in 1787 to the Present Time, Including the Services of Indiana Troops in the War with Spain*, Indianapolis, Ind.: W. D. Pratt, Printer and Binder, 1901.

Common militia units raised in this manner for federal service were restricted to use within the United States and for a maximum of three months, as stipulated in the 1792 Uniform Militia Act and thus bound to the Constitution's militia clauses. Binding Army expansion to the militia clauses complicated the federal government's efforts to expand the Army.

First, it meant that militia units formed under the 1792 Uniform Militia Act could not be used on foreign soil, because the Constitution allowed for the militia to be used only to enforce laws, suppress insurrections, and repel invasion. The Constitution said nothing about sending the respective states' common militias off to foreign lands (e.g., Mexico, European countries) to fight alongside the Regular Army, for example. If the various states disagreed with the purpose of the war or emergency (as the War of 1812 would eventually prove to be a significant issue), they had constitutional grounds to resist the federal call for militia units. They could do so by simply not meeting their federal quotas or refusing to allow their already organized compulsory militia units to be used for the war.

Another complicating factor for the federal government was that the 1792 Uniform Militia Act stipulated that, once federalized, a compulsory militia's term of service could not exceed three months. This reinforced state constitutions, laws, and traditions that held that three months was the longest amount of time a man could spend away from either his farm or other livelihood. This made it difficult for the federal government to train troops and retain them once trained.

State-Formed Volunteer Militias

In addition to the common militias, states could raise a second category of militia units, which we call *state-formed volunteer militias* for federal service. These were volunteer units that states organized using their militia systems in response to levies from the federal government. There was some question as to whether or not this type of unit could be used for service longer than three months and outside the United States. During the War of 1812, for example, it was understood that they were organized under the militia clause of the Constitution and the subsequent militia laws, meaning that they could not be mobilized for longer than three months and deployed beyond the country's borders (i.e., to Canada). But later, for the war with Mexico, Congress elected to sidestep these limits by bringing the militia units into federal service as individual volunteers vice militia units on the premise of the armies clause, thereby treating them as volunteer forces and not militias. The Civil War raised comparably fewer problems because Congress needed troops to suppress a domestic rebellion.

State-Sanctioned Volunteer Militias

We refer to third kind of volunteer militias as *state-sanctioned volunteer militias* for federal service. These entities, which existed in colonial times alongside the common militias, were entirely voluntary and self-organized, usually by men who were keen on the military life or the camaraderie of their units. Unlike the common militias and the state-formed militias, the states did not organize them, and the 1792 Uniform Militia Act did not apply to them. States did, however, provide them with charters and rely on them for law enforcement functions and to fulfill federal levies for militia units. These state-sanctioned volunteer militias did, after all, constitute something akin to a standing force, and they had a modicum of organization and skill, at least compared with common militia units built from scratch. They therefore played an important role in the early months of the Mexican War and throughout the American Civil War.

Civil War Volunteer Regiments, Union Army

A fourth category of 19th century militias—*Civil War volunteer regiments, Union Army*—was closely related to the *state-formed volunteer militias* that were used in the War of 1812 and the Mexican War. We place these Civil War volunteer regiments in a separate category mainly due to the sheer scale, in a comparative sense to previous wars, with which they were generated by the states for the Union Army. Whereas for the Mexican War the states generated about 50,000 volunteer units of this type, for the Union Army alone in the Civil War, the aggregate number reached close to 1 million men in these volunteer units.

Federal Volunteers for the Spanish-American War

A fifth category of American militia emerged in the last two years of the 19th century: *federal volunteers for the Spanish-American War.* This category of volunteers was distinctly different from the other two types of 19th century volunteer militias in that the states played no role in either using them or generating them for federal service. Instead, they were organized in 1898 in the territories of Arizona, New Mexico, and Oklahoma. These volunteer territorial units for the Spanish-American War received their authority to organize, equip, and train officers from the federal government, making them fundamentally different from the other two types of 19th century volunteer militias, which were ultimately creatures of the states.

To sum up, there were multiple kinds of militias and volunteer forces, with the dominant forms being the compulsory or common militias and two kinds of volunteer militias. One kind of volunteer militia was organized by the states as units for federal service as part of the state militia system and in response to federal levies—but treated as federal volunteers as soon as they were handed off to the federal government. The other kind of volunteer militia consisted of units organized outside the state militia system, although the states came to rely on these types of volunteer militias for local issues, and to respond to federal quotas for the Mexican and Civil Wars. From these three types of 19th century American militias, one can discern two militia traditions. The first was the compulsory militia tradition—the premise that all adult (white) males had to serve in state-organized militias. The second was the volunteer militia tradition.[2] Over time, the volunteer militia tradition would continue while the compulsory militia declined to the point of becoming irrelevant, and, as we shall see, the armies clause would grow in importance while the militia clause waned—even as it related to the modern, statutorily defined "organized militia," the National Guard of the several states. The Militia Table in Appendix A of this volume provides another explanation of 19th century militias.

The War of 1812

The United States was finally drawn into the Napoleonic Wars in 1812, and in subsequent decades the United States found itself in two other major engagements, the Mexican War and the Civil War. Each demonstrated the weakness of the framework established by the Constitution and the Acts of 1792, 1795, and 1807 with respect to the insufficient capacity of the Regular Army and the inefficiencies of the militia system. These experiences encouraged the professionalization of the Regular Army but did little to affect military policy. In the 19th century, the American Republic was still sheltered by the protective barriers of the Atlantic and Pacific Oceans and therefore could accept an anemic military characterized by low readiness and small numbers.

The War of 1812 revealed the structural weakness of the federal government's reliance on the states to generate militia units and volunteer forces. The system was slow and inefficient; although Regulars and militiamen fought (the vast majority being militias) for at least a portion of the war, the Army never totaled more than 70,000 men at any one time.[3] The failures in 1792 and 1795 to establish either a single training requirement or a mechanism to enforce state training and equipment standards ensured that the men who did fight in state-generated militia units often lacked sufficient preparation or arms.[4] Neither was the Regular Army in stellar shape at the beginning of the war; far from it. The Regular Army did have some experienced men, but

2 Jerry M. Cooper, *The Rise of the National Guard: The Evolution of the American Militia, 1865–1920*, Lincoln, Neb.: University of Nebraska Press, 1998; Mahon, 1983, pp. 110–111; Joseph John Holmes, *The National Guard of Pennsylvania: Policeman of Industry, 1865–1905*, PhD dissertation, Storrs, Conn.: University of Connecticut, 1971; Henry Martyn Boies, "Our National Guard," *Harper's New Monthly Magazine*, 1880; "A Brief History of the Oldest Minnesota National Guard Company," *National Guardsman*, May 1901; Martha Derthick, *The National Guard in Politics*, Cambridge, Mass.: Harvard University Press, 1965; Michael D. Doubler, *I Am the Guard: A History of the Army National Guard, 1636–2000*, Washington, D.C.: Army National Guard, 2001; Raymond F. Pisney, "The Brandywine Rangers in the War of 1812," Wilmington, Del.: Hagley Museum & Library, 1950.

3 Marvin A. Kreidberg and Merton G. Henry, *History of Military Mobilization in the United States Army, 1775–1945*, Washington, D.C.: Department of the Army, 1955, p. 50; Weigley, 1984, p. 121.

4 C. Edward Skeen, *Citizen Soldiers in the War of 1812*, Lexington, Ky.: University Press of Kentucky, 1999, pp. 4–16.

many of them were scattered on frontier duty.[5] The first battles of the War of 1812, especially, demonstrated significant weaknesses in both the Regular Army and state-generated militia units. The U.S. Army's overall relative weakness against a professional army was made humiliatingly clear in August 1814, when it was powerless to stop a well-trained British regular force of approximately 5,000 men from burning a number of buildings in the nation's capital, including the White House.[6]

When the war began, Congress increased the size of the Army by filling out the ranks of existing Regular Army regiments, building new ones through federal recruitment, authorizing the states to generate volunteer militia units, and setting quotas for the states to call forth their compulsory militias. The Regular Army at the start of the war consisted of 17 regiments of infantry, four of artillery, two of dragoons, one of riflemen, and a Corps of Engineers, all largely not geographically positioned to repel a British invasion. Because most of these formations had only recently been authorized, only a minority of them had much substance. The total authorized strength of the Regular Army was 35,603, and Congress voted to raise another 30,000 volunteers generated by the states under their militia systems, as well as asking state governors to ready 80,000 common or volunteer militiamen.[7]

The Regular Army never attained any of these numbers, in part because of uneven responses by state governments and counterproductive recruitment strategies that made efforts to raise volunteers for the federal forces compete with state militia recruitment. The War Department emphasized filling the ranks of the Regular Army through recruitment, in part because of the enduring view that militia could not be deployed to Canada. Indeed, the question of the legal status of using either federalized compulsory or volunteer militias for use against the British in Canada caused endless debate and frustrations for the federal government throughout the war. The Regular Army grew to an actual strength of only 15,000 by the end of 1812. In January 1813, Congress tried to expand the Army further by adding new regiments and boosting the authorized strength to 57,351, but it never reached those numbers in that year.[8]

In 1814, the war became more dangerous. Up to that point, Britain's primary focus had been on fighting France in Europe, keeping North America a relatively minor theater with comparably low numbers of troops. Napoleon's losses that year and his abdication in April meant that Britain could deploy veteran units to North America and

---

5 Coffman, 1986, p. 4; Kreidberg and Henry, 1955, p. 45.

6 Anthony S. Pitch, *The Burning of Washington*, Annapolis, Md.: Naval Institute Press, 2000; Pisney, 1950; Donald R. Hickey, *The War of 1812: A Forgotten Conflict*, Urbana, Ill.: University of Illinois Press, 2012, pp. 206–207; J. C. A. Stagg, *Mr. Madison's War: Politics, Diplomacy, and Warfare in the Early American Republic, 1783–1830*, Princeton, N.J.: Princeton University Press, 1983, pp. 428–432.

7 Weigley, 1984, p. 118; Kreidberg and Henry, 1955, pp. 44–45; Richard W. Stewart, *American Military History*, Volume 1: *The Forging of a Nation, 1775–1917*, Washington, D.C.: U.S. Army Center of Military History, 2009, pp. 132–134.

8 Weigley, 1984, pp. 119–121.

mount a much larger effort against the United States; Congress raised the authorized size of the Regular Army to 62,274 but continued to struggle to fill the ranks through recruitment into the Regular Army. The shortfalls were partly due to mixed popular support for an aggressive war beyond the U.S. border. More practically, men had little interest in the relatively low pay (half of what a laborer could make per month) and lengthy enlistments (five years). Few also were willing to submit to the harsh military discipline of the time, make do with inadequate and qualitatively poor equipment and supplies, and endure the perils of wartime service. More did join, probably because of the growing threat of invasion, which motivated Americans to sign up far more than did an offensive against Canada, and at the end of 1814 the Regular Army and the combined state militias each counted about 35,000 men. The U.S. military—two years after the start of the war—finally approximated the size and quality required to counter a determined British offensive.[9]

The various types of militia units that the states generated for federal service tended to be formed first as companies, then into regiments, and finally brigaded as militia units. The Army brigaded Regular Army regiments and militia regiments separately, although there were plenty of examples of the two fighting together, such as Major General Andrew Jackson's decisive defeat of the British Army at the Battle of New Orleans in January 1815.[10] The thinking at the time was that, since the several states each used different regulations for drill, equipping, and organization, it would be better not to mix them with Regulars who followed their own set of standards and guidelines.

One problem with the militias, both compulsory and volunteer, was the opposition of New England states to heeding the federal government's calls to mobilize militias to defend the coast, operate against the British in New England, and even take part in an invasion of Canada. The New England states also discouraged recruitment for the Regular Army. New England governors justified their inaction by arguing that the 1795 Calling Forth Act gave the President the power to call forth the militia in cases of "imminent danger of invasion," but the President had not declared that there was such a danger. The Massachusetts Supreme Court even argued that while the President had the authority to mobilize the militia in case of invasion or insurrection, he lacked the

---

9 13,000 veterans of the Napoleonic Wars arrived in Canada between Napoleon's exile and September 1814. When the two countries signed the peace agreement in December, the number had already reached nearly 52,000 (Weigley, 1984, p. 121; Alan Taylor, *The Civil War of 1812: American Citizens, British Subjects, Irish Rebels, and Indian Allies*, New York: Vintage Books, 2010, p. 325; Hickey, 2012, p. 183).

10 For analysis of the Battle of New Orleans, see Donald R. Hickey, *Glorious Victory: Andrew Jackson and the Battle of New Orleans*, Baltimore, Md.: Johns Hopkins University Press, 2015; Charles B. Brooks, *The Siege of New Orleans*, Seattle, Wash.: University of Washington Press, 1961; Robert S. Quimby, *The U.S. Army in the War of 1812: An Operational and Command Study*, East Lansing, Mich.: Michigan State University Press, 1997, pp. 807–859; Samuel J. Watson, *Jackson's Sword: The Army Officer Corps on the American Frontier, 1810–1821*, Lawrence, Kans.: University Press of Kansas, 2012, pp. 96–122; Walter R. Borneman, *1812: The War that Forged a Nation*, New York: Harper Perennial, 2004, pp. 271–293; Hickey, 2012, pp. 216–224.

authority to determine that an invasion or insurrection in fact was taking place—that authority rested with the governors alone. The British later invaded New England in 1814, obliging the Massachusetts governor to scramble to raise militia, although he refused to commit his militia to federal command. When he asked the War Department for help, the War Department more or less told him he was on his own.[11]

The difficulties in raising adequate numbers of militiamen, combined with the Regular Army's recruitment problems, encouraged policymakers such as Secretary of War James Monroe to rely more exclusively on the Regular Army. To fill the ranks of the Regular Army and increase the size of the state militias for local protection, Monroe recommended to Congress in 1814 that it pass legislation authorizing the federal government to draft men directly into the Regular Army or common militia units. Although Congress ultimately turned it down, Monroe's recommendation was an important first step in establishing the civic responsibility of virtually all American men to not only serve when called into the state militias but also when ordered into the federal Army, as part of what would come to be called the "national forces," and would be raised under the armies clause of the Constitution.[12]

The Calhoun Expansible Army Plan, 1820

In the years following the somewhat luck end of the War of 1812, policymakers, led most notably by John C. Calhoun, Secretary of War from 1817 to 1825, were more determined than their predecessors to improve the means for expanding the Army. Before the war, Calhoun already had made a name for himself as a leader of the "War Hawk" faction of Congress, which held a strong nationalist line and called for war against Britain to gain national respect. Calhoun wanted to prepare the nation for imminent battle with Britain, and beginning in 1811 he argued in a number of speeches and articles that the nation needed an "additional regular force." Calhoun was not successful in preparing the nation for war when it did come, but the experience of the War of 1812 galvanized his determination to endow the Republic with a more robust military capability. What he argued for now was to retain as much as possible the Regular Army's quality and quantity and also to focus on making it "expansible" rather than relying predominantly on militias to grow the force in wartime. Calhoun made the case in a report to Congress on December 12, 1820:

---

[11] Taylor, 2010, pp. 180–182, 415–417; Weigley, 1984, pp. 124–126; Mahon, 1950; Mahon, 1960; Stagg, 1983; Arthur M. Schlesinger Jr,. *The Imperial Presidency*, Boston, Mass.: Mariner Books, 2004, p. 36. For contemporary primary source documents on the New England militias question, see H. V. Ames, ed., *State Documents on Federal Relations: The States and the United States*, Philadelphia, Pa.: University of Pennsylvania, 1911, pp. 54–63.

[12] Jack Franklin Leach, *Conscription in the United States: Historical Background*, Rutland, Vt.: C. E. Tuttle Pub. Co., 1952; Leonard W. Levy, *Jefferson and Civil Liberties: The Darker Side*, revised ed., New York: Quadrangle, 1973; *History of Congress*, "War Measures," October 1814, pp. 483–496.

> However remote our situation from the great powers of the world, and however pacific our policy, we are, notwithstanding, liable to be involved in war; and, to resist, with success, its calamities and dangers, a standing army in peace, in the present improved state of military science, is an indispensable preparation. The opposition opinion cannot be adopted, without putting to hazard the independence and safety of the country. I am aware that the militia is considered, and in many respects justly, as the great national force; but, to render them effective, every experienced officer must acknowledge, that they require the aid of regular troops. . . . [T]o rely on them beyond this, to suppose our militia capable of meeting in the open field the regular troops of Europe, would be to resist the most obvious truth, and the whole of our experience as a nation.[13]

For Calhoun, it was imperative that the "great and leading objects" of a peacetime army

> ought to be to create and perpetuate military skill and experience, so that, at all times, the country may have at its command a body of officers, sufficiently numerous and well instructed in every branch of duty, both of the line and staff; and the organization of the army ought to be such as to enable the Government, at the commencement of hostilities, to obtain a regular force, adequate to the emergencies of the country, properly organized and prepared for actual service.[14]

Knowing that he and like-minded policymakers would never persuade Congress to pay for a large professional force, Calhoun hoped at least to protect and nurture a professional core in the Regular Army, complete with enough professionally trained officers to allow for the expansion of Regular Army regiments. He wanted the core to be just large enough so that it could be expanded, rapidly, without having to create additional new regiments—which would necessitate commissioning new officers with little to no expertise. It was, Calhoun argued, a grave error made in the previous war to rely on untrained militias with poorly led officers to expand the Army:

> This was the fatal error at the commencement of the late war, which cost the country so much treasure and blood. The peace establishment, which preceded it, was very imperfectly organized, and did not admit of the necessary augmentation; nor did the Government avail itself of even its limited capacity in that respect. The forces raised were organized into new corps, in which, consequently, every branch of military duty was to be learned by the officers as well as the men.[15]

---

[13] John C. Calhoun, *Report of the Secretary of War of a Plan for the Reduction of the Army of the United States (December 12, 1820)*, Referred to the Committee on Military Affairs, Washington, D.C.: Gales & Seaton, 1820, p. 4.

[14] Calhoun, 1820, p. 4.

[15] Calhoun, 1820, p. 10.

Secretary of War Calhoun insisted that it was preferable to reduce the strength of infantry soldiers in the regiments rather than reduce the total number of regiments:

> The propriety of reducing each regiment to its minimum force. . . . Rather than reducing the number of regiments, and making them somewhat stronger has been chiefly deduced from the following principle, the desire of avoiding to create new regiments, with raw inexperienced officers at their head, in the time of war.[16]

Calhoun wanted the Regular Army's infantry regiments in times of peace to be manned with enlisted soldiers at 50 percent strength yet have a full complement of officers and noncommissioned officers. Then, when war or crisis came, the existing regiments could be expanded rapidly with new individual volunteers drawn from the (white) male population, who would fall in with Regular Army soldiers and officers. This would allow the Regular Army to expand from a peacetime strength of around 6,000 to a wartime strength of 12,000. Calhoun's plan also provided for adding more soldiers and officers to the infantry companies after wartime strength had been achieved, thus increasing the overall size of the Regular Army to upward of 25,000 men. The essence of his plan was to scale up the Regular Army by filling out its ranks rather than having to create entirely new units or rely on the states to produce militia units for federal service.[17] In Calhoun's plan, the state militias would be dedicated to performing state duties and would not be required to expand the Regular Army. Importantly, Calhoun based his plan to expand the Regular Army on the armies clause of the Constitution, not the militia clause.

Calhoun's expansible army plan was built on some of the ideas of army expansion offered by Washington, Knox, and von Steuben in the years following the American Revolution. It represented a way of thinking among Regular Army officers that the proper military policy for the United States should be centered on the Regular Army and its expansion in wartime and less so on calling forth the state militias. Congress, however, rejected most of Calhoun's plan in its 1821 Army Reduction Act. In that law, Congress did allow for an enlisted strength at about 50 percent of authorized war strength, but without the full complement of cadre officers in each regiment and the reformed staff that Calhoun had recommended.

In the era of President Andrew Jackson, the country preferred to rely on the idea of the civilian-soldier and retained a powerful belief in states' rights.[18] Indeed, during

---

[16] Calhoun, 1820, p. 17.

[17] Calhoun, 1820; C. Vann Woodward, "The Age of Reinterpretation," *American Historical Review*, Vol. 66, No. 1, October 1960; Roger Spiller, "Calhoun's Expansible Army: The History of a Military Idea," *South Atlantic Quarterly*, No. 79, Spring 1980.

[18] As an example of this attitude, in a speech in 1826 about the troops he commanded during the War of 1812, Jackson venerated the character and comportment of volunteers, arguing that they were "the wealth and sinew" of America. These "were the citizen-soldiers, who appreciated, above all earthly blessings, the liberties achieved

the period from the end of the War of 1812 to the election of Abraham Lincoln to the Presidency in 1860, the one issue that loomed over all others was slavery, which today might be described as the "third rail" of American politics. Because Congress simply could not consider reforming the Regular Army and the militia system without tangling with the issue of states' rights, i.e., slavery, it would not take meaningful action. To pursue serious Army and militia reform would have meant that some states would have raised fears of too much centralizing authority under the federal government, not only through the Army but also through the state militia systems, which, in their minds, might be used to threaten the institution of slavery in the South. This was especially the case after the Mexican War ended in 1848 and the issue of what to do about slavery in the newly acquired territories from Mexico came to the fore. Ironically, though Calhoun's 1820 expansible Army plan would have centralized federal power, he became a strident advocate, until his death in 1850, of the right of Southern secession based on states' rights if the Union threatened the existence of slavery.[19]

Nonetheless, Calhoun's expansible army plan and its premise of a highly professionalized Regular Army persisted well into the first decade of the 20th century. What was new—and what would have an enduring impact—was a vision of the Army that saw little place for the state militias and that saw the Regular Army as being largely synonymous with *the* Army. Others disagreed, of course, either notwithstanding the experience of 1812 or because they interpreted the experience differently. In any case, many persisted in regarding the militias as the backbone of the Republic's defenses. This fundamental disagreement about the proper relationship and optimal balance between the Regular Army and the local militias would endure to the present.

In the meantime, the Army continued to stumble forward without a clear military policy, relying on ad hoc coalitions of Regular Army troops and militias. For example, in the second year of the Second Seminole War in Florida (1835–1842), Brigadier General Richard Keith Call assumed command of a total force that included 1,000 Regular Army troops and 250 Florida militiamen. Call tried to increase the size of the force by asking Tennessee to raise 1,000 volunteer militiamen (at this point, most states

---

by their fore-fathers, & had sworn to hand them down, unimpaired, to their children, or die in the attempt. With such an army your rights *could not* be infringed, nor your property molested." Jackson also celebrated their effectiveness, arguing that it "was the prowess of those citizen-soldiers, that enabled me so promptly and effectually, to terminate a savage war—to meet and vanquish their more savage allies," the British at New Orleans (Andrew Jackson, "Speech to William Pitt Martin and the Citizens of Fayettville, Tennessee [July 5, 1826])," in Harold D. Moser and J. Clint Clifft, eds., *The Papers of Andrew Jackson*: Volume VI: *1825–1828*, Knoxville, Tenn.: University of Tennessee Press, 2002, pp. 182–183).

[19] John G. Grove, *John C. Calhoun's Theory of Republicanism,* Lawrence, Kans.: University Press of Kansas, 2016; Frederic Bancroft, *Calhoun and the South Carolina Nullification Movement*, Baltimore, Md.: Johns Hopkins University Press, 1967; Daniel Webster and John C. Calhoun, *The Constitution Not a Compact Between Sovereign States: A Speech by the Hon. Daniel Webster in the Senate of the United States, Jan., 1833, in Reply to the Resolutions Offered by Mr. Calhoun, of South Carolina, Affirming the Right of Secession*, London: Woodfall and Kinder, 1862; August O. Spain, *The Political Theory of John C. Calhoun*, New York: Bookman Associates, 1951.

had, for the most part, done away with compulsory militia units and instead relied on volunteers to build new militia companies for federal service on the frontier) in two regiments. Tennessee complied, but when the Tennessee regiments moved through Alabama to reach Florida, they got caught up instead in a fight against Creek Indians. By the time they made it to Florida, their three-month enlistment was almost up. They threatened to leave, and eventually did.[20]

One important evolution of the militias that did take place during this period, as mentioned above, was that the common or compulsory militias had declined significantly, perhaps because the threat posed by Native Americans was now far removed for most Americans as the frontier moved rapidly west. By 1845, virtually all states had removed laws requiring active enrollment in the state common militias. However, as we shall see, while the common militias atrophied, volunteer militia units started to increase significantly. It was these volunteer militia units, along with individual volunteers formed into new units by several states to fulfill federal levies, that provided the bulk of the Army's expanded ranks in the Mexican War.[21]

The Mexican War (1846–1847)

On the eve of America's war with Mexico in 1845, the Regular Army was still relatively small, with an authorized strength of 8,619 soldiers and officers but an actual strength of approximately 6,560. Life as a frontier soldier was not consistent with the aspirations of most young Americans. By the spring of 1846, as hostilities appeared imminent, President James Polk ordered an "Army of Occupation" to form along the Texas-Mexico border. The "Army of Occupation" consisted of almost half of the Regular Army. Under the command of Brigadier General Zachary Taylor, this force of Regulars—organized in two brigades consisting of a total of five regiments of infantry, four regiments of artillery, and one regiment of dragoons—had distinct advantages compared with their peers in the War of 1812. First, virtually all of the company grade officers in the Regular regiments were West Point graduates, many of whom would later attain fame in the Civil War, such as Robert E. Lee, Ulysses S. Grant, George C. Meade, P. G. T. Beauregard, and many more. These West Point graduates proved especially helpful with their engineering and artillery skills. For example, during Commanding General Winfield Scott's march to Veracruz in 1847, one of his staff engineers, Captain Robert E. Lee, reconnoitered a route through the mountains and around the Mexican Army positions that Mexican Army leaders thought was impassable. Second, the men they commanded also happened to have been well trained and disciplined

---

20 Mahon, 2010.

21 Mahon, 1983; Cunliffe, 1968; William H. Riker, *Soldiers of the States: The Role of the National Guard in American Democracy*, Washington, D.C.: Public Affairs Press, 1957.

under a standard fighting doctrine written by General Scott. In other words, for perhaps the first time, the U.S. Army began a war with more than a modicum of professionalism and skill that previously American troops had to acquire on the job, often at a high price in terms of blood and treasure.[22] Unsurprisingly, the Regular Army performed well in the first two battles of the war in May 1846 at Palo Alto and Resaca de la Palma.[23] In both cases, it outfought the Mexican defenders, who suffered high casualties and retreated in disorder. Taylor's Regulars also evinced the ability to combine infantry, cavalry, and artillery. Of course, a number of limitations remained evident. Few field-grade officers had experience handling larger formations of battalions and regiments. Similarly, the three Regular Army general officers at the start of the war had no experience commanding brigades and divisions, as such formations were not required for frontier duty.[24] The biggest problem, however, was that the Regular Army was not big enough to accomplish tasks larger than what it was already doing.

The successful battles of Palo Alto and Resaca de la Palma incited Congress and much of the public to call for a formal declaration of war against Mexico, which Congress declared on May 13, 1846. Because it was obvious to Congress and the President that the Army would need to be much larger, they moved quickly to avail themselves of the legal mechanisms at their disposal to mobilize troops. Congress authorized the President to use the Regular Army and Navy, and also to expand the Regular Army by bringing infantry companies from a prewar strength of 42 privates per company to a war strength of 100 privates per company.[25] We see in this move an echo of Washington and Calhoun's ideas about expanding the Army by filling out the ranks of units that already had their full complement of officers and noncommissioned officers, rather than the time-consuming process of creating new units.

Yet this approach did not result in a Regular Army that was big enough for the task at hand. In May 1846, Congress authorized the President to call into federal service compulsory/common militia units from the several states for a period of six months.

---

22 See William B. Skelton, *An American Profession of Arms: The Army Officer Corps, 1784–1861*, Lawrence, Kans.: University Press of Kansas, 1992; Samuel J. Watson, *Peacekeepers and Conquerors: The Army Officer Corps on the American Frontier, 1821–1846*, Lawrence, Kans.: University of Kansas Press, 2013; Timothy Johnson, *Winfield Scott: The Quest for Military Glory*, Lawrence, Kans.: University Press of Kansas, 1998; Allan Peskin, *Winfield Scott and the Profession of Arms*, Kent, Ohio: Kent State University Press, 2003; Francis Paul Prucha, *The Sword of the Republic: The United States Army on the Frontier, 1783–1846*, New York: Macmillan, 1969; James L. Morrison Jr., *"The Best School": West Point, 1833–1866*, Kent, Ohio: Kent State University Press, 1998; Coffman, 1986; Weigley, 1984, pp. 174–175.

23 Stephen A. Carney, *Guns Along the Rio Grande: Palo Alto and Resaca de la Palma*, Washington, D.C.: U.S. Army Center of Military History, 2005; Henry Lee, *The Militia of the United States: What It Has Been, What It Should Be*, Boston, Mass.: Marvin & Son, 1864.

24 Richard Bruce Winders, *Mr. Polk's Army: The American Military Experience in the Mexican War*, College Station, Tex.: Texas A&M University Press, 1997, pp. 32–49.

25 Winders, 1997, p. 9; Edward Deering Mansfield, *The Mexican War: A History of Its Origins*, New York: A. S. Barnes & Co., 1849, p. 26.

However, Congress and the President used only limited numbers of these forces, for border defense in states such as Louisiana, because of the constitutional restriction of using militias on foreign soil. In the same act, Congress therefore authorized the President to bring into federal service 50,000 volunteers, with a term of service for either one year or "for the duration" of the war, with the states or the volunteers to decide.[26]

As for what kind of militia, the act deferred the question to the states, which pulled together various combinations of volunteer militias, using whatever means and procedures they saw fit. As the act put the matter:

> [T]he said volunteers so offering their services shall be accepted by the President in companies, battalions, squadrons and regiments, whose officers shall be appointed in the manner prescribed by law in the several states and territories to which such companies, battalions, squadrons, and regiments respectively belong.[27]

Again, unlike the War of 1812, Congress brought the volunteer units, even the ones organized by the states, into federal service under the armies clause so that they could be sent to Mexico. All told, by the end of the war in 1848, the War Department reported that there were 73,260 men in federal service in volunteer companies and regiments, although the total number of volunteers on active service at any time was never more than 50,000.[28]

The trajectory of the Mississippi Rifles Infantry Regiment provides a good illustration of how state-sanctioned militias served in the Mexican War. The regiment formed in Mississippi as a volunteer militia in 1799 and saw service in the War of 1812. When Congress in May 1846 authorized the President to bring on 50,000 volunteers for federal service to fight in Mexico, Mississippi offered up the Mississippi Rifles as part of its contribution. The Mississippi Rifles, then commanded by Colonel Jefferson Davis, a West Point graduate and future president of the Confederacy, joined General

---

[26] Robert W. Johannsen, *To the Halls of the Montezumas: The Mexican War in the American Imagination*, New York: Oxford University Press, 1988; K. Jack Bauer and H. Sutton James, Jr., *The Mexican War, 1846–1848*, New York: Macmillan, 1974, pp. 57–58; Kreidberg and Henry, 1955, pp. 70–72; James M. McCaffrey, *Army of Manifest Destiny: The American Soldier in the Mexican War, 1846–1848*, New York: New York University Press, 1992, p. 16; Weigley, 1984, p. 183; John S. D. Eisenhower, *So Far from God: The U.S. War with Mexico, 1846–1848*, Norman, Okla.: University of Oklahoma Press, 2000, p. 88.

[27] "An Act Providing for the Prosecution of the Existing War Between the United States and the Republic of Mexico (Approved May 13, 1846)," in John F. Callan, ed., *The Military Laws of the United States*, Philadelphia, Pa.: George W. Childs, 1863, p. 368. There was precedent for this. This language was used verbatim in legislation a decade before the Mexican War for the Creek War of 1836. Other language was altered slightly. The 1836 legislation called for no more than 10,000 volunteers to serve six or 12 months "only in cases of Indian hostilities or to repel invasions, whenever the President shall judge proper. . . ." For the most part, the 1836 legislation seems to be a clear blueprint for 1846 (Callan, 1863, p. 366).

[28] Weigley, 1984, p. 183; Winders, 1997, p. 72.

Taylor's forces in northern Mexico in the fall of 1846 and played an important role in the Battle of Buena Vista in February 1847.[29]

Another example is a unit formed in Indianapolis, Indiana, by a young lawyer named Lew Wallace (who would later attain fame as a Union general in the Civil War). To attract the interest of local men looking to volunteer under the May 1846 act calling for 50,000 volunteers, Wallace hung a banner outside his law office with the words "For Mexico, fall in." Within three days, Wallace's volunteer militia company was full, and it elected him its lieutenant. It was then folded into a volunteer regiment, which the state of Indiana offered to the federal government as part of its quota. A few months later, Wallace's company converged on the Mexican border with thousands of other volunteer militiamen formed in similar ways to reinforce Taylor's regulars and take the fight into Mexico.[30]

As the war progressed, and as Taylor pushed farther south into Mexico, the proportion of volunteers to Regulars shifted until roughly only 30 percent of the overall force consisted of Regulars, with 70 percent volunteers. The Regulars often were critical of the volunteers and disdainful of their training and their discipline. There certainly were problems. First, Scott and Taylor thought it necessary to hold the volunteer units back and subject them to additional training before sending them across the U.S.-Mexico border to join the front. Second, the volunteers tended to be sticklers when it came to their terms of service, which in many cases were short. Scott had to stop halfway in his drive from Vera Cruz to Mexico City because the one-year service term of 4,000 volunteer militiamen in his ranks ended. Scott had to send them home and wait in the middle of a hostile country for three months for reinforcement by a new group of "for the duration" volunteers.[31] Like all armies, health problems afflicted U.S. forces in Mexico, but a greater proportion of volunteers reportedly were invalided by sickness than Regulars.[32] The Regulars alleged that the problem was the volunteers' poor food and sanitation practices on the march and in camp. There were also allegations of problems with discipline. Volunteer units reportedly were more prone to riot and to commit atrocities against Mexican civilians.[33] Taylor wrote candidly in September 1846 that "The whole system of volunteers at best is defective but [made] much worse than it might be" because of mismanagement from within the volunteer ranks "by those who control it for political effect, which is the case in present instance." Even their presence was ill-advised, because volunteers "were never intended to invad[e] or

[29] Richard Bruce Winders, *Panting for Glory: The Mississippi Rifles in the Mexican War*, College Station, Tex.: Texas A&M University Press, 2016a.

[30] Lew Wallace, *Lew Wallace: An Autobiography*, Vol. 1, New York: Harper & Brothers Publishers 1906, pp. 114–120; Winders, 1997, p. 71.

[31] Weigley, 1984, pp. 183–184; Stewart, 2009, pp. 186–190; McCaffrey, 1992, pp. 165–204.

[32] Mahon, 1983, p. 92.

[33] Mahon, 1983, p. 95.

carry on war out of the limits of their own country, but should be used as the constitution intended," defending the nation from invasion and enforcing law and order.[34]

In total, some 26,922 men served in the Regular Army, and another 73,260 served in the volunteer units.[35] Scott and Taylor, though they had reduced expectations of the volunteers and managed to get good performance out of them, and by and large the volunteers acquitted themselves well on the battlefield. Given their numbers, one cannot imagine a victory without them. The greater professionalization of the Regular Army probably helped: There were quite simply more and better trained officers and noncommissioned officers (including former soldiers now serving in the militias) around to teach the volunteers, get them up to speed, and provide new units with a measure of competent leadership.[36] Indeed, Grant in his memoirs noted that volunteers were "without drill or discipline at the start"; however, "they were associated with so many disciplined men and professionally educated officers, that when they went into engagements it was with a confidence they would not have felt otherwise.[37]

The relative success of the volunteers was such that the war emboldened both sides of the old debate between the so-called professionalists and the militia advocates. Those who believed in the virtues of professional soldiers saw evidence of their value, tended to stress the limitations of the militias, and generally believed that the war effort might have gone more smoothly had the Regular Army been able to conduct the war without recourse to volunteers—in other words, had the Army been large enough to do the job mostly on its own. Militia advocates, on the contrary, took heart in the speed with which the militias mobilized and acquired the proficiency required to meet the nation's needs. Ultimately, the pro-militia view, which predominated before the war, continued to hold sway, but the professionalist school persisted and continued to characterize the views of Regular Army officers and others interested in military policy. A good example is the work of Mexican War veteran and West Point graduate Henry Wager Halleck. Halleck made a name for himself before the war by publishing a thorough study of America's coastal fortifications.[38] He subsequently refocused

---

34 William K. Bixby, *Letters of Zachary Taylor from the Battlefield of the Mexican War*, Rochester, N.Y.: The Post Express Printing Co., 1908, p. 51.

35 Bauer and James, 1974; Weigley, 1984, p. 183; Richard Bruce Winders, "Race and Republicanism: Understanding the Mindset of Mexican War Soldiers," in Geoffrey W. Jensen, ed., *The Routledge Handbook of the History of Race and the American Military*, New York: Routledge, 2016b, p. 41.

36 Skelton, 1992; K. Jack Bauer, "The Battles on the Rio Grande: Palo Alto and Resaca de la Palma, 8–9 May 1846," in William Stoft and Charles Heller, eds., *1776–1965, America's First Battles*, Lawrence, Kans.: Kansas University Press, 1984; Ulysses S. Grant, *Personal Memoirs*, New York: The Modern Library, 1885.

37 Grant, 1885, p. 84.

38 H. W. Halleck, *Report on the Means of National Defence*, Washington, D.C.: U.S. Government Printing Office, 1843.

his efforts on what many historians have termed "professionalism."[39] In 1846, he published *Elements of Military Art and Science*, which became the standard textbook on strategy for cadets at West Point. In this work, Halleck argued that American soldiers needed to receive specified training and studies just as other vocations received codified instruction:

> [A]n army usually obtains its recruits from men totally unacquainted with military life. . . . If years are requisite to make a good sailor, surely an equal length of time is necessary to perfect the soldier; and no less skill, practice and professional study are required for the proper direction of armies . . .[40]

Halleck also advocated for methodical field tactics over brash decisionmaking, thus supporting the view that good military leadership was a trained skill rather than some innate attribute that one might possess without any professional training.

Halleck left the Army in the 1840s, worked as a California land prospector, and served as a general in the California militia. When the Civil War broke out, he returned as a volunteer officer. He served primarily as Lincoln's Army Chief of Staff, responsible for the management of the Union Army during the Civil War.[41]

The Civil War (1861–1865)

On the eve of the Civil War, the nation had a larger Regular Army than before the Mexican War—roughly 15,000 enlisted men and officers at the beginning of 1861. Most were still scattered about the West in numerous posts or manned coastal fortifications.[42] By that time, the compulsory or common militias organized under the 1792 Uniform Militia Act were largely in poor condition or had disappeared altogether. Most states could muster only a small proportion of the total number of eligible and enrolled citizens.[43] States used these in a number of capacities and roles. California, for example, deployed its state militia to suppress Native Americans under the guise of

---

[39] Russell Frank Weigley, *The American Way of War: A History of United States Military Strategy and Policy*, New York: Macmillan, 1973, pp. 84–91; Skelton, 1992, pp. 241, 246; Brian Linn, *The Echo of Battle: The Army's Way of War*, Cambridge, Mass.: Harvard University Press, 2007, pp. 23–24.

[40] H. W. Halleck, *Elements of Military Art and Science; or, Course of Instruction in Strategy, Fortification, Tactics of Battles, &c.; Embracing the Duties of Staff, Infantry, Cavalry, Artillery, and Engineers. Adapted to the Use of Volunteers and Militia*, New York; Philadelphia, Pa.: D. Appleton & Co.; G. S. Appleton, 1846, p. 144.

[41] John F. Marszalek, *Commander of All Lincoln's Armies*, Cambridge, Mass.: The Belknap Press of Harvard University Press, 2004; Weigley, 1973, pp. 119–152.

[42] Skelton, 1992, p. 135.

[43] Kreidberg and Henry, 1955, p. 90; Mahon, 1983.

aiding miners in the Gold Rush. The period also saw several interstate militia conflicts, such as the so-called Utah or Mormon conflicts.[44]

There were some regional differences of note that became important when the war broke out. In the North, generally only a few states in the northeast had militias of any substance, in particular a number of state-sanctioned volunteer militias. This left the North at a disadvantage when the war broke out and the federal government called on the states to form militias: The North had relatively fewer military leaders with experience or training. In contrast, the South had a relatively more robust militia system, owing to historical concern with policing slaves, tracking runaways, and preventing or crushing revolts.[45] The net result was a proportionately larger number of men with military experience available to serve newly formed Confederate regiments.

When the war broke out in April 1861, President Lincoln initially called for 75,000 militiamen for three months of federal service to secure the capital and other key locations. These militiamen came from virtually all northern states as newly organized state common (compulsory) militia units, volunteer militia companies, and individual volunteers. Their immediate availability in a matter of weeks, and sometimes days depending on the proximity of northeastern states to Washington, D.C., and northern Virginia, was immensely valuable to Lincoln, because it bought him time to consider and pursue more-substantive measures. Their effectiveness was limited, though, in part because few of the men serving had ever drilled with a unit. These were the men who fought and lost the first major battle against Confederate forces at the first Battle of Bull Run in July 1861.[46]

In the months that followed the first mobilization, Lincoln, with Congress's eventual approval, repeatedly called on the states to form new volunteer regiments manned by three-year volunteers. By August 1861, the War Department reported that 486,000 three-year volunteers in state-formed regiments were in service.[47]

Based on advice he received from the commanding general of the Army, Winfield Scott, Lincoln decided to keep the Regular Army, and particularly its officers and noncommissioned officers, together in Regular Army units.[48] It may have made more sense to distribute these Regular Army officers and noncommissioned officers to newly

---

[44] David Goodman, *Gold Seeking: Victoria and California in the 1850s*, Stanford, Calif.: Stanford University Press, 1994, p. 186; William P. MacKinnon, *At Sword's Point, Part 1: A Documentary History of the Utah War to 1858*, Norman, Okla.: The Arthur H. Clark Company, 2008; William P. MacKinnon, *At Sword's Point, Part 2: A Documentary History of the Utah War, 1858–1859*, Norman, Okla. University of Oklahoma Press, 2016; Coakley, 1989, pp. 194–226.

[45] Sally E. Hadden, *Slave Patrols: Law and Violence in Virginia and the Carolinas*, Cambridge, Mass.: Harvard University Press, 2001; H. M. Henry, *The Police Control of the Slave in South Carolina*, Emory, Va., 1914.

[46] Kreidberg and Henry, 1955, pp. 90–93; Weigley, 1984, pp. 198–199; James M. McPherson, *Battle Cry of Freedom: The Civil War Era*, New York: Oxford University Press, 1988, p. 274.

[47] Weigley, 1984, p. 200.

[48] Kreidberg and Henry, 1955, p. 97.

forming volunteer regiments so they could teach the untrained soldiers and officers, but the distaste among the militias of being commanded by Regular Army officers should not be underestimated. Because the Confederacy had no regular army, the Confederate government did the opposite by dispersing the former Regular Army officers who resigned their commissions to fight for the South (e.g., Robert E. Lee, Stonewall Jackson, and James Longstreet) out to the newly formed Confederate regiments. Arguably, this was one of the reasons the Army of Northern Virginia during the first year of the war consistently outperformed the Union's Army of the Potomac, although the quality and performance of the Confederate regiments varied by the respective states that raised them.[49]

Scott's advice to President Lincoln was indicative of the professionalist mindset that held sway among Regular Army officers. For Scott, the key to Union success in the Civil War lay with a highly trained and potentially expanded Regular Army. In a way, Scott was refighting the Mexican War. He believed that the Regular Army, reinforced by limited numbers of volunteers, would provide an offensive arm capable of penetrating the Confederacy and defeating its army, just as he had done in Mexico in 1847. Scott failed to grasp the revolutionary nature of the Civil War—that it was a war not just to defeat an enemy army and government, but a war to defeat people committed to the cause as well. He thus underestimated the scale to which the conflict would soon rise.

As the war ground on, the Union struggled to keep the Army at full strength, which it did through 1861–1862 with repeated calls to the state governors to form more volunteer units. One issue in particular had to do with replacements: Should they be used to fill out the ranks of extant regiments decimated by fighting or be used to form new ones? The more common approach was to create new ones, which had negative consequences: Veteran regiments became too small to be of use because of attrition, while the new regiments lacked combat experience and, absent the guidance that might have come from veteran officers and men, had to learn how to fight the hard way. By the time they learned their trade, they often resembled the smaller veteran units.[50]

For example, Maine in May of 1861 formed the 4th Maine Volunteer Infantry Regiment and placed it under the command of Colonel Hiram G. Berry. After mustering out of Rockland, Maine, the regiment counted 1,085 men. The 4th Maine went on to fight in numerous battles, from Bull Run to Cold Harbor in 1864. Out of the original 1,085, 443 were wounded, 137 succumbed to disease, 170 were killed in action,

---

[49] John McAuley Palmer, *America in Arms: The Experience of the United States with Military Organization*, New Haven, Conn.: Yale University Press, 1941.

[50] Leonard L. Lerwill, *The Personnel Replacement System in the United States Army*, Washington, D.C.: Department of the Army, 1954.

and 40 died in Confederate prison camps.[51] Rather than replenish the regiment, Maine in 1864 transferred the surviving soldiers to a newly formed regiment, the 19th Maine Infantry.

Because states struggled to reach their recruiting objectives, Congress in July 1862 directed state governors to use their authority per the 1792 Uniform Militia Act to draft men into newly forming regiments for federal service. The 1862 law notably dropped the word "white" from the description of the class of men between the ages of 18 and 45 liable to serve—a deliberate break from the 1792 Uniform Militia Act—and also authorized enlisting African-Americans and granted freedom to escaped slaves who did labor for the Army or joined its ranks.[52] Governors never put the law into effect, partly because they managed, after all, to meet their recruitment quotas. However, in March 1863, Congress passed a second conscription law—the Enrollment Act.[53] Congress intended the Enrollment Act to do two things. First, Congress hoped to spur voluntary enlistment; unlike draftees, volunteers received bonuses and could choose their regiments.[54] Second, Congress wanted men to reinforce units already in federal service. The Enrollment Act worked as intended. Enlistments in newly forming volunteer units surged because men thought they were a better option than being drafted. Those who were drafted helped replenish Union Army units.

There were two related aspects of the 1863 Enrollment Act of note. First, the conscription system prescribed by the act bypassed state governments: The law called for federal officials operating draft offices in congressional districts and drafting men directly into federal service. One negative consequence was that the federal draft provoked violent protests in New York City in the summer of 1863.[55] The cause apparently was not conscription in and of itself but the fact that now the federal government was

---

51 William B. Jordan, *Maine in the Civil War: A Bibliographical Guide*, Portland, Maine: Maine Historical Society, 1976, p. 60.

52 U.S. Statutes at Large, An Act to Amend the Act Calling Forth the Militia to Execute the Laws of the Union, Suppress Insurrections, and Repel Invasions, 1862. Also see the amendment to this act that authorized replacements and bounties: U.S. Statutes at Large, An Act to Amend an Act Entitled "An Act for Enrolling and Calling Out the National Forces, and for Other Purposes, " Approved March Third, Eighteen Hundred and Sixty-Three, Thirty-Eighth Congress, Session I, Chapter 13, February 24, 1864 (13 Stat. 6).

53 U.S. Statutes at Large, An Act for Enrolling and Calling Out the National Forces, and for Other Purposes, Thirty-Seventh Congress, Session III, Chapter 75, March 3, 1863 (12 Stat. 731).

54 William Best Hesseltine, *Lincoln and the War Governors*, New York: A. A. Knopf, 1948; Leach, 1952; Fred A. Shannon, *The Organization and Administration of the Union Army*, Bethesda, Md.: University Publications of America, 1994; William L. Shaw, *The Civil War Federal Conscription and Exemption System*, Washington, D.C.: Judge Advocates Association, 1962a; Eugene C. Murdock, *Patriotism Limited, 1862–1865: The Civil War Draft and the Bounty System*, Kent, Ohio: Kent State University Press, 1967; Eugene C. Murdock, *One Million Men: The Civil War Draft in the North*, Madison, Wisc.: State Historical Society of Wisconsin, 1971.

55 Iver Bernstein, *The New York City Draft Riots: Their Significance for American Society and Politics in the Age of the Civil War*, New York: Oxford University Press, 1990; Allan Nevins, *The War for the Union: War Becomes Revolution, 1862–1863,* Volume I, New York: Scribner, 1959.

doing it directly, removing local control of the process. The act also talked about the militias in a novel way. Whereas the 1792 Uniform Militia Act and the 1862 law presumed to be talking about state militias raised and organized by state governments, the Enrollment Act spoke of "all men" constituting the "national forces." It reads:

> Be it enacted by the Senate and House of Representatives of the United States of America in Congress assembled, That all able-bodied male citizens . . . between the ages of twenty and forty-five years, except as hereinafter excepted, are hereby declared to constitute the *national forces*, and shall be liable to perform military duty in the service of the United States when called out by the President for that purpose.[56] (Emphasis added.)

The Enrollment Act stipulated that all able-bodied men between certain ages were now part of the "national forces" and thus liable for "military duty" to the United States—not the states, but the United States (i.e., the states were no longer part of the equation). The law established a direct link between the federal government and the individual very different from that envisioned by Congress in 1792 when it passed the Uniform Militia Act.

As a result of these various means for acquiring manpower, the Union Army comprised several different types of soldiers:

- soldiers in the Regular Army
- men who joined state-sanctioned volunteer militias
- men who joined state-formed volunteer regiments
- men drafted into federal service.

There were also men who served in militia units at home who never passed into federal service. These, in some cases, were called forth for local defense, which is what happened with the Pennsylvania militia during Lee's invasion in the summer of 1863.[57] In total, the number of units required by the Union and even Confederacy dwarfed what the prewar militia structure could provide, and the overwhelming number of

---

[56] U.S. Statutes at Large, An Act for Enrolling and Calling Out the National Forces, and for Other Purposes, 1863; James W. Geary, *We Need Men: The Union Draft in the Civil War*, DeKalb, Ill.: Northern Illinois University Press, 1991.

[57] As one example, when Lee's army invaded Pennsylvania in 1863, local militia companies were mustered for a period of six months, and provided about 20,000 soldiers for defense of the state. For Confederate militia, see Kreidberg and Henry, 1955, pp. 129–137; Albert Burton Moore, *Conscription and Conflict in the Confederacy*, New York: Macmillan, 1924, pp. 1–11; William C. Harris, *Leroy Pope Walker: Confederate Secretary of War*, Tuscaloosa, Ala.: Confederate Pub. Co., 1962, pp. 56–71; William L. Shaw, "The Confederate Conscription and Exemption Acts," *American Journal of Legal History*, Vol. 6, October 1962b; E. Merton Coulter and Frank L. Owsley, "The Confederate States of America, 1861–1865," *Journal of Economic History*, Vol. 10, No. 2, 1950. For the Confederate Army, see Joseph T. Glatthaar, *General Lee's Army: From Victory to Collapse*, New York: Free Press, 2008.

soldiers who served in the Union Army came in as new volunteers in state-formed regiments.

Conclusion

With the conclusion of the Civil War, the evidence available at the time suggested strongly that the system worked, at least insofar as it enabled the nation to generate and sustain enormous armies when required. There was a significant time delay between when Lincoln called for forces and adequately trained and equipped units became available, but, up to that point, few had cause to think unacceptable the risk associated with that delay. This is not to say that nothing had changed or needed to be changed: The 1863 Enrollment Act, for example, represented an important change in military policy by moving away from the militia clause and embracing the armies clause as the best means to generate large land forces. Moreover, the common or compulsory militias, which had been the backbone of the nation's military power at the end of the 18th century and beginning of the 19th, had diminished greatly in importance. The militia tradition at the end of the Civil War was alive and well, only it was the volunteer militias that had become predominant.

CHAPTER FIVE

Attempts at Army Reform: The Post–Civil War Years to the Spanish-American War

Introduction

After the Civil War, the Army predictably shrank in size. The old debate between professionalists and militia advocates resumed, although in this period it evolved in important ways. On the professionalist side, wartime experience and multiple developments in the nature of warfare both at home and abroad encouraged a number of theorists—foremost among them former Brevet Major-General Emory Upton—to update Calhoun's arguments in favor of an expansible army that relied on a federal reserve rather than state militias. At the same time, however, the 1870s saw the beginning of a renaissance among the nation's state-sanctioned volunteer militia units, which increasingly referred to themselves as National Guards (after the French). These units took on greater importance as a result of their (often unpopular) role in law enforcement and dealing with civil unrest, but they also evolved into a politically active body that advocated in favor of being officially recognized as central to the nation's defenses. During this period, there was halting progress toward an informal compromise between the professionalists and the militia/Guard advocates that translated into growing acceptance of the place of the National Guards of the states in the national defense as a potential reserve force for Army expansion, with increased federal support. However, some Guard advocates worried that this increasing federal support might compromise their cherished links to state governments.

Post–Civil War Developments: The Rise of the Modern National Guards

At the close of the Civil War in 1865, the Army, comprised of a small number of Regular Army units and substantially larger volunteer forces, shrank rapidly, just as it had after previous wars. The total Union Army had reached a peak of 1,000,000 at war's end, yet it was under 200,000 within a year; through the Reconstruction period, the Regular Army's strength was less than 60,000, with about 19,000 of its soldiers involved in policing the southern states.[1] Militias in both the North and the South more or less ceased to exist, including state-sanctioned volunteer militia units. The men who had served in them had no desire to perform further military service after four years of bloody warfare.[2] The federal government, moreover, was of mixed mind regarding militias in the South. It variously encouraged black militias while discouraging white ones that were judged likely to consist of Confederate veterans, only to end up allowing ex-Confederate militias as time passed and the federal government's commitment to Reconstruction wavered. Black and white militias coexisted in the 1870s, with occasional clashes and bloodshed, the most notorious incidents being the so-called Colfax Massacre of 1873 and the Battle of Liberty Place of 1874. Eventually, southern states, once again under Democratic Party control, disbanded black militias altogether. The demise of the black militias in the south in the 1870s was part of southern whites' reassertion of control.[3]

The 1870s also marked the revival of state-sanctioned volunteer militias, now almost universally known as National Guards. These grew in strength and number and, perhaps more importantly, earned increased support from state governments and eventually even the federal government, which appreciated the Guards' value as standing military forces available for use to deal with civil disturbances, such as labor unrest and race riots. One contributing factor was the growth in unrest associated with industrialization and the rise of the labor movement, particularly in the northeast. Another was Posse Comitatus, the law passed by Congress in 1878 at the request of southern leaders to limit the Regular Army's ability to intervene in local domestic, civil matters (and thereby end the Army's role in defending southern blacks from southern whites intent on reasserting their control). Posse Comitatus did not end interventions by the Regular Army, but it enhanced the value to governors of alternatives, i.e., National Guard units. In any case, the state-sanctioned volunteer militia units were certainly busy. According to one count, governors summoned their Guardsmen 481 times between the Civil War and 1906. Most instances had to do with labor unrest, but racial violence was an important driver, particularly in southern states: According to the same source, governors called out the Guard 59 times to intervene in lynchings, 30 more times to quell additional trouble between blacks and whites, and twice (in California) to put down anti-Chinese riots.[4]

---

1 Stewart, 2009, p. 304; Weigley, 1984, pp. 265–267; John C. Sparrow, *History of Personnel Demobilization in the United States Army*, Washington, D.C.: Department of the Army, 1952, pp. 5–8.

2 For works on civilian and military life after the war, see James Marten, *Sing Not War: The Lives of Union & Confederate Veterans in Gilded Age America*, Chapel Hill, N.C.: University of North Carolina Press, 2011; Brian Matthew Jordan, *Marching Home: Union Veterans and Their Unending Civil War*, New York: Liveright Publishing Corporation, 2014; Jack D. Foner, *The United States Soldier Between Two Wars: Army Life and Reforms, 1865–1898*, New York: Humanities Press, 1970.

3 Mahon, 1983, p. 110.

4 Mahon, 1983, p. 110. Cooper (1998, pp. 44–64) cites different statistics that corroborate Mahon.

The increased use of the state volunteer militias for domestic purposes and the growing support from state and later federal governments encouraged a growing self-awareness among Guard members and their supporters, who began to assert their collective interests and promote the role of the state National Guards in the nation's defense. Essentially, the new National Guard units and their leaders began to push back against the idea that their primary mission lay in internal law enforcement, which had become increasingly unpopular. They preferred to be soldiers, not law enforcement officers or strike breakers, and they also began to demand better organization and training. Increasingly calling themselves the "National Guard" and modeling themselves after Regular Army formations, they also began to insist that their primary role was as a reserve force to the Regular Army in the "first-line defenses." They wanted to receive more funding from the federal government and be less reliant on state funding, and they argued that this expenditure was a more effective investment than an equivalent investment in the Regular force. In support of these ideals, the National Guard Association formed in 1878 to lobby for changes in the militia system.[5]

Many of the senior National Guard leaders who established the National Guard Association remembered the difficult Civil War experience of procuring sufficient manpower for the Union and Confederate armies. Looking back to the mix of volunteerism and conscription in both the North and South, Guard leaders in the decades following the Civil War embraced the tradition of the civilian-soldier who volunteers for militia service. As military historian Jerry Cooper aptly summarized, in addition to being seen as a fighting force of the first line, the Guards in the decades following the Civil War also sought "legislative recognition as the volunteer reserve for the nation" and the premise that the National Guards embodied "the volunteer citizen soldier."[6] To be clear, they were wary of too much federal control. What they wanted, in effect, was to be regarded by the federal government as the heart of the nation's defenses and the Regular Army's reserve and to be the beneficiary of federal materiel support and training, all the while retaining their status as state forces under state control.

But for the volunteer vision of these Guardsmen to be put into practice, Congress would need to revise the outdated 1792 Uniform Militia Act. However, in the years between the end of Reconstruction in 1877 and the war with Spain in 1898, few in the United States paid much attention to military policy, and even state politicians who favored an increasingly important role for the Guards in state and national defenses were unwilling to commit to the Guard forces a large amount of taxpayers' dollars. Many Americans at that time thought that war was behind them and that the two

---

5 Holmes, 1971; Boies, 1880; "A Brief History of the Oldest Minnesota National Guard Company," 1901; Derthick, 1965; Doubler, 2001, pp. 104–106.

6 Jerry Cooper, *The Militia and National Guard in America Since Colonial Times: A Reference Guide*, Westport, Conn.: Greenwood Press, 1993, p. 87.

oceans separated them from other conflicts around the world; as such, updating the military policy for the Army seemed, again, to be irrelevant and unnecessary.

The Influence of Emory Upton and the Expansible Army Concept

Although most of the country turned away from questions of military policy during the decades following the Civil War, former Brevet Major-General Emory Upton played a major role in post–Civil War military tactics and reform. Upton's work focused on pragmatic and detail-driven studies. He abandoned the traditional American-centric perspective and focused on international comparative studies as the basis of his scholarship. His intent was to transform the U.S. military into a force fit to defend the United States from foreign powers, nations that were building armies of increasing size and lethality. Upton's research would take him around the globe and culminate in his most famous, albeit posthumous, work, *The Military Policy of the United States.*[7]

In 1866—after five years of distinguished combat service in the Union Army, where he earned a reputation for brilliant combat leadership and tactical innovation—Upton was sent to West Point to lead a group of Regular Army officers there in revising infantry tactics. As a result of his work at West Point, Upton published *A New System of Infantry Tactics* in 1867.[8] The new tactical method for American infantry took into account modern developments, as well as new battlefield technologies, such as the breach-loading Prussian "needle gun." Indeed, Upton and others understood that warfare was entering a new stage, as superior weaponry was beginning to make Civil War tactics, such as marching and forming close ranks, suicidal. Upton studied the battles of the German wars of unification while also drawing on his own experience as a combat leader in the American Civil War.[9]

---

7 Upton, 1903. For a thorough but incomplete collection of Upton's writings, see Peter Smith Michie and James Harrison Wilson, *The Life and Letters of Emory Upton*, New York: Arno Press, 1979. Also see David Fitzpatrick, *Emory Upton: The Misunderstood Reformer*, PhD dissertation, Ann Arbor, Mich.: University of Michigan, 1996; David Fitzpatrick, "Emory Upton and the Citizen Soldier," *Journal of Military History*, April 2001. Stephen Ambrose's work remains the standard for those seeking a biographical depiction of Upton: Stephen E. Ambrose, *Upton and the Army*, Baton Rouge, La.: Louisiana State University Press, (1964) 1993. For an interpersonal and theological perspective, see Jeffrey Neale Hice, *The Utmost Devotion to Duty: Rediscovering the Faith and Character of General Emory Upton*, Allegany, N.Y.: St. Bonaventure University, 1996. The Upton letters and manuscripts from the Hagley Museum and Library and U.S. Army Heritage and Education Center at Carlisle Barracks were also consulted.

8 Emory Upton, *A New System of Infantry Tactics, Double and Single Rank, Adapted to American Topography and Improved Fire-Arms*, New York: D. Appleton, 1868.

9 Many have traced the origins of the "professional army" to Prussia. See Samuel P. Huntington, *The Soldier and the State: The Theory and Politics of Civil-Military Relations*, Cambridge, Mass.: Belknap Press of Harvard University Press, 1957.

In 1878–1879, the Commanding General of the Army, Lieutenant General William Tecumseh Sherman, sent Upton on a worldwide expedition to survey and live among the major armies of the world. The resulting publication was *The Armies of Asia and Europe*.[10] The text examines in detail a number of nations' order of battle and their mobilization schemes, use of regular troops and reserves, approach to professional military education, and staff planning. In a lengthy "Conclusions" section, Upton listed a number of what might today be called "lessons learned" or "best practices" on how other nations organized their ground forces. His list betrays his own preference for the Prussian military, which he clearly held in the highest regard. Of particular interest to him was its tiered corps of regulars and different kinds of reserves, its capacity to expand quickly, and its deep commitment to military education and professionalization, which, among other things, guaranteed that the officers who led hastily mobilized units filled by reservists or new recruits knew their business and were highly qualified to lead their men into battle. Moreover, the better European armies filled the ranks of their depleted battalions, rather than create new ones, enabling new soldiers to benefit from the expertise of the surviving veterans.[11] Of course, Upton's real interest was in comparing the European armies with the U.S. Army, a comparison that, in Upton's view, placed in sharp relief the flaws of the ad hoc American method of Army expansion:

> If we now compare our military policy during the first century of the Republic with the present military policy of European nations, we shall find that the difference lies principally in this—that, while they prosecute their wars exclusively with trained armies, completely organized in all of their parts, and led by officers specially educated, we have begun, and have prosecuted, most of our wars with raw troops, whose officers have had to be educated in the expensive school of war.[12]

Upton was convinced that the United States consequently paid a high price in casualties because the relative ineptitude of American forces, at least at the beginning of conflicts, translated into long, protracted wars, whereas, in comparison, the Europe-

---

[10] Emory Upton, *The Armies of Asia and Europe: Embracing Official Reports on the Armies of Japan, China, India, Persia, Italy, Russia, Austria, Germany, France, and England*, Portsmouth, England: Griffin & Co., 1878.

[11] Upton, 1878. Although Weigley's 1962 *Towards an American Army* is still a very useful intellectual history of the U.S. Army, Weigley is perhaps a bit too critical toward Upton's views and does not really place them within the context of Upton's times. Taking a similar approach to Weigley is Ambrose, (1964) 1993. For a hypercritical view of Upton that misrepresents many of his ideas and casts him in an unfair light, see Jim Dan Hill, *The Minute Man in Peace and War: A History of the National Guard*, Harrisburg, Pa.: Stackpole Books, 1964. For more-current scholarly treatments of Upton, see Fitzpatrick, 1996, 2001; and J. P. Clark, *Preparing for War: The Emergence of the Modern U.S. Army, 1815–1917*, Cambridge, Mass.: Harvard University Press, 2017.

[12] Upton, 1878, p. 321.

ans seemed capable of bringing quick conclusions to their conflicts at a relatively low price.

Upton proposed two alternative plans. The first was to organize and nationalize the Regular Army in such a way that "by the mere process of filling out its ranks of enlisted soldiers, it may be expanded to such proportions as to enable it, without other aid, to bring our wars to a speedy conclusion."[13] Upton, in fact, was offering an updated version of Calhoun's "expansible" army scheme, one that for the most part bypassed the states. In Upton's view, the states should certainly maintain their militia forces—and he even penned a short book on simple military tactics for the militias to use—but they had no business in providing untrained men to fill out the ranks of the Regular Army or of raw volunteer units like in the Civil War.[14] Instead, in this plan by Upton, the federal government would run replacement training centers throughout the states, based on population size and demographics.

The second plan was to prosecute future wars by relying on volunteer troops supplemented by regular artillery and cavalry, and by distributing regular officers among the volunteer units to provide them professional leavening. Both plans could work, he argued, provided that there was a division of the country into military regions with regional recruitment and training, the creation of a general staff, the establishment of a War Academy to promote military education for higher-ranking officers, and a number of other steps inspired primarily by the Prussians.[15]

As for relying on the states to produce militia units to expand the Regular Army, Upton argued that the current system was inadequate, partly because the states seldom contributed enough money to make the state militias of any value. Upton proposed as a substitute the creation of "one or two battalions of National Volunteers" attached to each of the 25 Regular Army regiments. These would be federal forces maintained at a relatively high state of readiness and capable of quickly filling out the Regular regiments. Militias would also exist, according to Upton's scheme, but they would not be relied upon for the nation's defense and would not be expected to play much of a role until after receiving training and perhaps benefiting from the presence of professional officers.[16]

---

13 Upton, 1878, p. 323.

14 Upton was disdainful of the loss of life during the Civil War because of some officers' blind obedience to obsolete tactics. The Army adopted *Infantry Tactics* in August 1867. His innovative instructions included advising infantry to fight in one or two ranks, urging individuals to employ intuitive thinking rather than mindless automatism, and advocating for rifled weapons.

15 Upton, 1878, p. 323.

16 Upton, 1878, p. 368; Andrew Bacevich, "Emory Upton: A Centennial Assessment," *Military Review*, December 1981. Also see Eliot Cohen, *Making Do With Less, or Coping with Emory Upton's Ghost*, Carlisle Barracks, Pa.: U.S. Army War College, 1995.

Upton's most controversial work was the posthumous *The Military Policy of the United States*,[17] written at the behest of General Sherman and later published in 1902 by Secretary of War Elihu Root (discussed in more detail in the second volume of this series). The intent of the original draft was to trace military policy from antiquity to the United States and to prescribe a professionalized military force with a complete severing of all previous ties to the states and their governors. Yet his own hands would not complete it: Upton took his life in 1881 in San Francisco.[18] Following his death, many recognized his historical and pragmatic approach toward policy reform and praised his work.[19]

In *The Military Policy of the United States*, Upton was more pointed in his criticism of the state militia systems used to expand the Regular Army in wartime, criticism that partly derived from his analysis of their role in the Civil War and America's other conflicts. According to Upton, part of the problem was simply the role of state governments and their large role in providing the federal government with local militias and individual volunteers to expand the Army when what the Union needed most was to bring a large, decisive force to the conflict with the Confederacy. He noted with irony that the system was designed to protect liberties but ultimately failed to do so both by getting people needlessly killed (by protracting the war) and by obliging the government to compel citizens to serve. After all, he reasoned, had Lincoln been able to "bring 10,000 regulars upon the battlefield of Bull Run," no one would have needed to be compelled to serve. Instead, "the first success of the insurgents having made their aiders and abettors bold and defiant, no other course was left open, except to subject them to the pains and penalties of military law."[20]

Upton, moreover, was scornful of the idea of relying on militias—undertrained and not led by competent officers—and was concerned that America's past military successes misled people into thinking that the established way of mobilizing military strength was sufficient. His aim in writing *The Military Policy* was to disabuse the public of what he considered to be a significant misconception:

> History records our triumph in the Revolution, in the War of 1812, in the Florida War, in the Mexican War, and in the Great Rebellion. . . . [A]nd as nearly all of

[17] Upton, 1903.

[18] Hice, 1996, pp. 221–244; Ambrose, (1964) 1993, p. 148; Clark, 2017, p. 127.

[19] Richard C. Brown, "General Emory Upton—The Army's Mahan," *Military Affairs*, Vol. 17, No. 3, 1953; Richard Barry, "Emory Upton, Military Genius—Practically Unknown General, for Whom Camp at Yaphank Was Named, Advocated Many Years Ago Reforms Embodied in Our Great Army of Today," *New York Times*, June 16, 1918, pp. 2, 59.

[20] Upton, 1903, p. 428; R. M. Cheseldine, "Where Emory Upton Made His Big Mistake," *Infantry Journal*, March 1930.

> these wars were largely begun by militia and volunteers, the conviction has been produced that with us a regular army is not a necessity.[21]

The problem with this record, according to Upton, was that it obscured "the delays and disasters" that characterized those campaigns, "the unnecessary sacrifice of life and treasure, which has attended all our armed struggles."[22] In fact, in Upton's estimation, much of the blame lay with the militia system of the several states. "In the Revolution," he wrote, "the Continentals or Regulars often displayed a valor deserving of victory, but which was snatched away by the misconduct of undisciplined troops."[23] Upton devoted much of *The Military Policy* to recounting the failings of American military policy in general and the country's unwise reliance on militias in particular. A representative example was the failure to defend Washington, D.C., in 1814, which Upton said happened precisely the same way as the failure to defend Philadelphia during the Revolution:

> In both cases the enemy approached by the Chesapeake; in both cases Congress and the President, as the Chief Executive of the nation, turned to the states for assistance; in both cases, instead of calling the troops in the field when the enemy's object was first discovered, Congress and the President sought to economize by inviting the States "to hold the militia in readiness to march at a moment's notice;" in both cases, when the critical moment arrived, the militia was powerless in the presence of a disciplined force, and in both cases the want of an adequate regular army caused the capital to fall into the hands of our enemies.[24]

As we shall see, Upton's idea of an expansible army was never implemented, but many of his arguments would inform the professionalists and reformists for decades to come and thus shape at least one half of the debates over military policy. One was the desirability of a federal reserve completely outside state political influence. Another was the conviction, which would grow in time, that the complexities of modern warfare demanded still greater professionalization: The amount of time required to turn raw civilian recruits into proficient soldiers was growing.

Military historian Graham Cosmas, writing about the Army at the dawn of the Spanish-American War, argues that both the professionalists and the militia advocates

---

21 Upton, 1903, p. vii.

22 Upton, 1903, p. vii.

23 Upton, 1903, p. xi.

24 Upton, 1903, p. 129. For a contemporary view of U.S. Army officer attitudes toward the problem of expansion and U.S. military policy, see U.S. Senate, Joint Committee on the Reorganization of the Army, *Report to Accompany S.1491*, 45th Congress, 3rd Session, S. Rep. 555, December 12, 1878.

were stumbling toward something of a compromise.[25] On one hand, he writes, supporters of the Regular Army increasingly understood that they would get neither an expansible Regular force nor a federal reserve, meaning that they would have to focus instead on making the Guards of the states as "well regulated" as possible. Ideally, the Guards of the states might acquire many of the attributes that the professionalists sought in a federal reserve if subject to greater federal control (and furnished more federal dollars, which would purchase that control). For their part, Guard advocates were warming up to a significantly closer relationship with the federal government and Regular Army, all the while protecting zealously their affiliations with their home states and their governments.

Conclusion

The roughly 30 years between the Civil War and the Spanish-American War were a time of transition, when state-sanctioned volunteer militias, increasingly referred to as National Guards, began emerging as a de facto reserve for the Regular Army, even though the extant laws (still governed by the 1792 Uniform Militia Act) made no such provision. In addition, there was still no formal relationship between the federal government and Regular Army and the National Guards of the states. Professionalists (and reformists) led by Upton continued to argue for the necessity of a strong Regular Army, the comparative disadvantage of state militias led by inexperienced officers, and the very idea of civilian-soldiers. The evolution of military technology helped them make their case, even if the nation's security requirements at the time made the idea of a large standing force out of the question. Militia advocates-cum-National-Guard proponents, in turn, saw the National Guards of the states as the inheritor of the volunteer civilian-soldier ideal, and they believed the Guards should be the principal source of manpower and organized units to expand the Army when foreign and domestic threats arose. U.S. military policy itself, however, would not change until the Spanish-American War forced the matter into public debate.

---

[25] Graham A. Cosmas, *An Army for Empire: The United States Army in the Spanish-American War*, College Station, Tex.: Texas A&M University Press, 1998, p. 45.

CHAPTER SIX

The United States Enters the World Stage: The Army and the Spanish-American War

On the eve of America's war with Spain, the nation's Regular Army was poorly organized and largely unprepared to fight. In 1898, it totaled around 28,000 men, largely dispersed throughout the western United States in the remaining frontier outposts.[1] It was not uncommon for companies in the Regular Army regiments to be isolated in outposts, thus making it difficult to centralize units for training. The Regular Army by 1898 had replaced its older single-shot, black-powder-firing Springfield rifles with more advanced, magazine-fed Krag-Jørgensen rifles, which fired smokeless powder rounds. It had also replaced its old muzzle-loading smoothbore, black-powder-firing cannon with rifled breech-loading guns. But because Congress had appropriated too little money, the Regular Army had no reserve stocks of either, and barely enough smokeless powder to supply the weapons it did have. Army tactics had also evolved, to some degree, in response to the new technology. For example, because of the greater range and accuracy of modern rifles, the Regular Army was moving away from close ranks and learning to trust captains, other lower-ranking officers, and noncommissioned officers to operate in smaller, dispersed groups. Nonetheless, there were many new skills the Regular Army had yet to master, including the large-scale maneuvers with synchronized combined arms.

The state volunteer militias, now known as National Guards, were probably in better shape than they had ever been, thanks to growing state and federal support. However, Guard units retained obsolete, black-powder-firing weapons and defaulted to what amounted to Civil War–era tactics. Moreover, they varied tremendously in quality from unit to unit and from state to state, and they had little to no experience working with the Regular Army, or a desire to do so. Neither the Regular Army nor the National Guards of the states had experience conducting large-scale maneuvers. The biggest problem, of course, was that the Army was not large enough to fight a war, and certainly was not prepared for one. Past experience had demonstrated that this was, for the most part, fine: America's ad hoc system of mobilizing volunteers to fill the ranks of

---

[1] Kreidberg and Henry, 1955, pp. 149–150.

coalitions of federal and state regiments and rushing them to war had been sufficient, albeit also expensive in terms of blood and treasure. Mobilization might have taken more time than anyone would have liked, but that, too, was fine, given that the nature of the threats the nation faced did not really require better.

In some regards, the Spanish-American War confirmed the validity of the above. The nation, as we shall see, managed to cobble together forces adequate to do the job, and in fact to a large extent suffered from mobilizing too many people. Still, the combined military forces of the United States delivered a crushing defeat against Spain in Cuba. Yet a variety of problems stemming from the limitations of contemporary military policy made for a shocking spectacle of an Army unprepared to fight an inferior force, let alone deploy it outside the continental United States in numbers that the nation had never experienced.

Part of the problem was the timing. The United States went from neutrality in the war between Spain and Cuban insurgents to mobilization to a declaration of war and then to invasion in only a few months. This short time frame would have strained any military, or at least any military that did not have a Prussian-style mobilization system such as the one brought to bear against France in 1870. Another problem was the fact that President William McKinley kept changing his strategic objectives, which affected directly the question of how many troops Washington would require, for what purpose, and where and how they would fight. During the scramble to mobilize for the war amid changing objectives, professionalists and Guard advocates each offered rival plans. Worse, because there still was no formal policy regarding who would reinforce the Regular Army and how, the mobilization ended up being a multiparty negotiation involving the War Department, Congress, the National Guards, and state governments, each with their own agendas.

First, and in response to McKinley's original intentions, which required a relatively small force, Uptonian advocates for the Regular Army proposed legislation that came to be known for its sponsor, Representative John Hull. The idea behind the Hull bill was that an expanded Regular Army would be sufficient for fighting the war and offered the most effective tool for doing so. It proposed to establish an "expansible" army that presumably would have been large enough to avoid having to summon the state National Guards. The bill proposed focusing the National Guard on coastal defense. The Guards of the states, however, wanted to secure a central role in the nation's military, including significant participation in the looming conflict with Spain. Through its friends in Congress, the National Guards of the states successfully blocked passage of the Hull bill. In the words of a pro-Guard Pennsylvania congressman,

> By this bill . . . the United States infantry will almost, if not entirely, supplant the National Guard—that now valuable auxiliary to our national strength.
>
> The aftereffects of such a bill can be easily foreshadowed. The probabilities of the National Guard being called into service, after this bill becomes law, will be

> exceedingly remote, and will cause interest in the Guard to lag. This Guard will lose its importance in the eyes of the people, and rightly or wrongly, will fall into oblivion and disappear as an efficient and inexpensive mainstay.[2]

The death of the Hull bill left war planners with a problem: They still did not have the means to mobilize a force large enough to invade Cuba. The administration naturally fell back on the classic approach of summoning the states to produce volunteer National Guard forces. Following the April 22, 1898, Volunteer Army Act, in which Congress authorized the President to summon militias for federal service, McKinley called for 125,000 volunteers under the new law, even though the War Department had anticipated a call for only 60,000. The reason for overshooting the mark was that McKinley faced intense pressure from the state Guards; their relatively new lobbying arm, the National Guard Association; and state governments to, in effect, ensure that as many Guard units from as many states as possible could participate.[3] The Cuban expeditionary force consisted originally of 14,412 Regulars and 2,465 volunteers, the latter in the Rough Riders and two famous National Guard regiments, the 2nd Massachusetts and 71st New York. Reinforcements arriving at the front after the principal fighting was over raised the total of volunteers to 7,443.[4]

Interestingly, the 1898 Volunteer Army Act repeated the 1863 Enrollment Act's use of the term *national forces*. The 1898 act reads:

> [A]ll able bodied male citizens of the United States . . . between the ages of eighteen and forty-five years, are hereby declared to constitute *national forces*, and, with such exceptions and under such conditions as may be prescribed by law, shall be liable to perform military duty in the service of the United States.[5]

The act also went another step toward creating a federal reserve by calling for the creation of three federal volunteer regiments that would form entirely outside of state control and pass directly into federal service. They all formed in the Western territories

---

[2] Quoted in Cosmas, 1998, p. 88.

[3] The 125,000 figure was equally a signal of resolve to Madrid, according to Graham A. Cosmas, "From Order to Chaos: The War Department, the National Guard, and Military Policy, 1898," *Military Affairs*, Vol. 29, No. 3, Autumn, 1965, pp. 118–119; and Kreidberg and Henry, 1955, p. 156. The McKinley administration held out hope that Spain might still capitulate without a fight. The decision to opt for 125,000 instead of the anticipated 60,000 volunteers also allowed McKinley to avoid Lincoln's mistake of calling out too few troops at the outset of war (Cosmas, 1965, pp. 105–122; Clark, 2017, pp. 167–168).

[4] David A. Clary and Joseph W. A. Whitehorne, *The Inspectors General of the United States Army, 1777–1903*, Washington, D.C.: U.S. Army Center of Military History, 1987, p. 362.

[5] U.S. Statutes at Large, An Act to Provide for Temporarily Increasing the Military Establishment of the United States in Time of War, and for Other Purposes, Fifty-Fifth Congress, Session II, Chapter 187, April 22, 1898 (30 Stat. 361).

to make sure they skirted state government interference, although men from across the nation joined their ranks. One of those regiments, the 1st United States Volunteer Cavalry, would gain renown during the war as the "Rough Riders" under the leadership of future U.S. President Theodore Roosevelt and command of Colonel Leonard Wood, a future Chief of Staff of the Army.

Congress passed subsequent legislation that allowed the states to fill their quotas by providing entire National Guard units. However, to avoid complications associated with a call-up of the National Guard under the Constitution's militia clause, the soldiers in these units voted to determine whether they would be federalized as a unit or took individual oaths and were essentially inducted under the armies clause of the Constitution. As a further recognition of the increasing importance of the National Guards as state-organized, but still federally unrecognized, reserves, President McKinley also asked first for volunteers from the organized militias (i.e., the preexisting state Guards), stipulating that he would receive additional men only when organized units fell short of a state's quota. Once called to federal service, these state Guard units were under strength, like the Regular Army units, and needed individual volunteers to fill out their ranks to war strength.[6]

Organizational and equipping differences between Regular Army and state National Guard units exacerbated the problems with the Army's mobilization. Although the state National Guards, by and large, were better equipped and trained in 1898 than previously, thanks to growing state and federal support and general professionalization, they comprised little more than an aggregation of mostly unrelated state military forces. They suffered from a lack of uniformity of instructions, training, equipment, and organization. No standardized system for selecting officers existed; it was still common practice in some states for Guard units to elect their own officers. State and federal funds were also generally scarce among Guard units, as was sufficiently trained leadership.[7] Moreover, age limits for enlisting in various Guard units often differed from those of federal units. They also had, at the outset of the war, none of the new weapons fielded by the Regular Army, specifically the Krag-Jørgensen rifles and breech-loading rifled artillery. They went to war with black-powder-firing Springfields and muzzle-loading smoothbore cannons. The Army prevailed on the battlefield, but in many ways the fight against the Spanish was harder and bloodier than many had imagined, largely because of the Spaniards' modern rifles, which made Civil War tactics too dangerous, and because American forces, for a variety of reasons, did not do as good a job as they might have of leveraging their strengths, conducting large-scale

---

6 Weigley, 1967, pp. 296–297.

7 Jerry M. Cooper, "National Guard Reform, The Army, and the Spanish-American War: The View from Wisconsin," *Military Affairs*, Vol. 42, No. 1, January 1978; Todd P. Frederick, "Our National Guard: An Introduction to Its History," *Military Affairs*, Vol. 5, No. 3, 1941; Kenneth Roy Bailey, *A Search for Identity: The West Virginia National Guard, 1877–1921*, dissertation, Ohio State University, 1976.

maneuvers, or making use of, for example, supporting artillery. Logistical problems prevented the Army from using all the guns it had, and the American military was not yet proficient in combined arms warfare, such as coordinating indirect fire in support of infantry. U.S. forces still relied on direct fire, which required bringing artillery up to the front, a dangerous thing to do when the enemy possessed modern weapons. Theodore Roosevelt summed it up well when he wrote of the fierce battle at San Juan Hill—which the Army won but at a cost that convinced Army commanders that they faced a much greater force than they actually did:

> We have won so far at a heavy cost; but the Spaniards fight very hard and charging these entrenchments against modern rifles is terrible. We are within measurable distance of a terrible military disaster.[8]

The course of the war also brought to the fore another problem: National Guard units in general tended to be infantry-heavy, and light on supporting arms such as artillery and cavalry, and all but bereft of what today are called combat support and combat service support capabilities. What the Army needed desperately when it invaded Cuba and, soon after, the Philippines and Puerto Rico were engineers and logisticians. It needed mule teams and wagoneers. It needed transport vessels and landing craft. It needed medical services. All of these things the War Department had to scramble to pull together and provide to the invasion forces. It eventually did, but not without confusion, inefficiency, and waste, some of which slowed down and weakened the Cuban campaign in particular. In the case of medical services, what little the Army managed to provide to the Cuban expedition collapsed when the invasion force fell sick *en masse* to malaria, yellow fever, typhoid, and dysentery, which had the combined effect of destroying the invading army *after* it defeated the Spanish. Comparable, though less severe, outbreaks swept through the large camps on the mainland, where mobilized volunteers had been concentrated to wait for deployments that never came. Reportedly, the volunteers were particularly prone to disease because they were less disciplined regarding camp sanitation.[9] A total of 21,000 contracted typhoid alone, affecting over 90 percent of the volunteer regiments, with the death toll among them reaching 1,800, compared with 751 Regulars. In total, about 2,500 died from sickness.[10]

---

8 Quoted in Cosmas, 1998, p. 218.

9 Cosmas, 1998, p. 268.

10 Cosmas, 1998, p. 278.

Demobilization and the Occupation

The need to occupy Cuba, Puerto Rico, and, above all, the Philippines, where soon the Army faced a new war, prevented the same kind of radical demobilization that occurred after the country's previous wars. The Republican McKinley administration continued to need manpower. In November 1898, it tried to win authorization for expanding the Regular Army to 100,000, which it reckoned would be sufficient for the Army's new imperial duties. The bill failed because of lingering resistance to the idea of a large standing army and the Democrats' opposition to annexing the Philippines, which the expanded Army was intended to support.[11]

However, the compromise bill that passed on March 2, 1899, authorized McKinley to maintain the Regular Army at 65,000, supplemented by a force of 35,000 federal volunteers (i.e., not National Guard or state-formed militias) until July 1901, when the Regular Army end strength would have to decrease to 30,000. This was essentially a stopgap measure. Nonetheless, it reflected the strength of Uptonian sentiment in favor of the Regular Army. The Army, moreover, had now evolved into something rather different than what it was before the war. It had become an expeditionary force with greatly improved combat support and combat service support capabilities, among them significantly better logistical capabilities and a fleet of ocean-going troop transports, landing craft, lighters, etc. These new strengths were on display after the Philippine-American War broke out in earnest in February 1899, when the Army not only had to reinforce troops there but also swap out the Spanish-American War volunteers with well-equipped and well-trained federal volunteer regiments authorized by the March 1899 act.[12]

Conclusion

Ultimately, the federal government's ad hoc approach to raising a war army once again proved sufficient to meet the nation's war objectives, albeit again inefficient, chaotic, and unnecessarily expensive in terms of lives and treasure. However, the Regular Army and volunteer units that deployed to Cuba to defeat the Spanish were not adequately equipped, trained, or prepared for the conditions and enemy they faced. The travails of the Spanish-American War would soon spur major reforms of the Army and, finally, changes to military policy.

---

[11] Cosmas, 1998, p. 305.

[12] On the logistical effort and the exchange of Spanish War veterans for new volunteers, see Cosmas, 1998, pp. 312–313.

CHAPTER SEVEN

Volume Conclusion

The American military that emerged with the foundation of the Republic and endured through the end of the 19th century was never an optimal fit for the country's security needs, but rather a compromise—indeed a set of compromises—between opposing points of view in a debate informed and constrained by American political culture. Many, perhaps even most, Americans rejected the idea of maintaining a large standing army under central authority because they considered it a threat to their liberty and was largely unaffordable anyway. At the same time, they tended to believe not only in the sufficiency of local militias, which dated to the beginning of Britain's colonization of North America, but also, for ideological reasons, that militias were consonant with American democracy.

Within that context, there emerged two camps. One, associated first with the Federalists and later with Secretary of War John C. Calhoun and Brevet Major-General Emory Upton, is often referred to as the "professionalist" camp. It favored trusting the burden of the nation's defense to a professional Regular Army. Because they understood that the nation would never agree to a large standing Regular Army, they envisioned instead a federal reserve, or some scheme that at least would hold state militias to common standards of discipline and proficiency. The other camp, which originally was common among critics of a standing army, favored the militia system and viewed state militias as adequate to meeting the needs of America's security. The militia advocates resisted efforts to expand the Regular Army and sought to guarantee the militias' status as the principal reserve of the Regular Army.

Throughout the 19th century, one thing that remained constant was the small size and generally anemic state of the Regular Army. In each of the wars the Army faced, from the War of 1812 to the Spanish-American and Philippine-American Wars, the federal government had to seek militia and volunteer forces to supplement the Regulars. Some things changed, namely the nature of the militias. Over time, the compulsory or common militias that were the mainstay of late 18th century America became defunct and were eclipsed by two forms of volunteer militias. *State-formed* volunteer militias were organized by the states in response to levies from the federal government. *State-sanctioned* volunteer militias were self-organized groups of volunteers that received state charters and to which the states learned to turn to extinguish labor strikes and quell riots. After the Civil War, these latter volunteer militias became widely known as National Guards of the several states. These National Guards, though they did not win the formal status they sought until after the Spanish-American War, nonetheless grew in strength and political influence. The National Guard aligned itself politically with the formation of the National Guard Association, which helped it gain recognition and support, first from state governments and increasingly from the federal government as well.

Another change was a gradual shift away from dependence on the states to provide militias, which was originally based on the militia clause of the Constitution, toward a federalization of the entire process and a recasting of the militias in terms of the armies clause. Congress during the Civil War, for example, authorized a draft directly into the federal service, whereas the 1792 Uniform Militia Act defined conscription purely in terms of state efforts to generate militias. For the Spanish-American War, Congress increased the federal role over the process in which the states produced volunteer National Guard units and went a step further, authorizing what amounted to federal volunteer militias raised and organized entirely outside state political influence.

The ad hoc system of cobbling together militia and volunteer forces to expand the Army beyond the meager Regular Army was marginally adequate: The nation won its 19th century wars, although most were more costly than many envisioned necessary. There was plenty of waste and inefficiency, facts noted by professionalists who continued to see evidence for the centrality of a professional Regular Army, with reduced dependence on militias for national security. However, the continuing resistance to large standing armies in American political culture, coupled with the lack of any compelling need for a robust peacetime military capability, kept military policy largely frozen in place for nearly a century. Only after the Spanish-American War—as discussed in the next volume—did the nation's leadership, with congressional support, act to reform military policy to meet an altogether different set of security requirements posed by the new century.

APPENDIX A

Summary Table of 19th Century Militias and Volunteer Forces

Table A.1 summarizes the various types of militias and volunteer forces that existed in the 19th century.

Table A.1
Summary Table of 19th Century Militias and Volunteer Forces

Type of Force	Organization	Legal Basis	Use	Period of Existence	Links to Present Day
Militia manpower pool	Was not organized and is referred to in current law as the "unorganized militia." It comprised all free able-bodied males between 18 and 45 years of age.	1792 Uniform Militia Act and state laws stipulating all adult free men's liability for militia service.	Was the manpower base for the various militias described below, both voluntary and compulsory.	Originated in the first American settlements in Virginia and Massachusetts and runs to the present day.	Title 32 (The National Guard) and Title 10, Subtitle A (The Army) both stipulate that American men ages 18–45 are in the "unorganized militia."
Compulsory or common militias	Individual states required all men to be on militia musters and to meet for training as part of a militia company of approximately 60 men several times per year. Militia companies were often formed into regiments. By state and federal law, the common militia's service was limited to 3 months.	1792 Uniform Militia Act and state laws stipulating all adult free men's liability for militia service.	States used the compulsory militias for local law enforcement, defense, and fighting against Native Americans. In times of war or insurrection, the federal government would assign quotas to states for militia units. Local militia captains would muster their men and organize a small number of volunteers or conscripts. The newly formed militia unit would be in federal service for up to 3 months.	Began in the first American settlements of Virginia and Massachusetts but had severely atrophied to the point that fewer and fewer states required men to muster regularly for training; by the 1840s, compulsory militia muster drill was a rarity, especially in the North.	None.

Table A.1—continued

Type of Force	Organization	Legal Basis	Use	Period of Existence	Links to Present Day
State-sanctioned volunteer militias for federal service	Men interested in military affairs and the camaraderie of other like-minded men formed volunteer militia units independent of the state-generated common militias. They could be used in federal service for longer than 3 months.	State and local laws authorized governors, mayors, magistrates, etc., to utilize volunteer militia units. Their service on foreign soil during the Mexican-American War was founded on the Constitution's "raise and support armies" clause because they were brought into federal service as individual volunteers.	These volunteer militias were often called on by state governors for a variety of uses, including law enforcement and the escorting of dignitaries. Equally important, state governors offered these volunteer militias to meet federal quotas for the Mexican-American War and the Civil War.	The first volunteer militia was established in Boston in 1638. More developed in the 18th century. Volunteer militias were used extensively in the Mexican-American War and were the first militia units to respond to President Lincoln's call in the spring of 1861. Starting in the late 1870s, new volunteer militias began to form and call themselves "Guards" or "National Guards," increasingly under state control.	The modern National Guard traces its historical roots to the volunteer militias that emerged in the 1870s after the Civil War.
State-formed volunteer militias for federal service	The federal government issued calls to states to organize a quota of volunteers into regiments for federal service. These volunteer militias could serve for longer than 3 months in times of war.	1792 Uniform Militia Act, state militia laws, and the Constitution's "raise and support armies" clause.	Volunteer militias were used inconsistently during the War of 1812, but constitutional barriers to their use beyond U.S. borders limited their utility. During the Mexican-American War, volunteer militias were locally organized, but the states could use them to meet federal quotas in times of war for 1–3 years.	The apex for volunteer militias and volunteer forces was during the Civil War, when the early armies of the war from the North and South consisted overwhelmingly of volunteer units.	None.

Table A.1—continued

Type of Force	Organization	Legal Basis	Use	Period of Existence	Links to Present Day
Civil War volunteer regiments, Union Army *(The sheer number of volunteers relative to other U.S. wars makes this a separate category.)*	Through Lincoln's executive order, the federal government issued quotas to states for "volunteers." States then relied on local systems to organize regiments of infantry, cavalry, artillery, etc. These volunteer units were technically "militias" because, under the 1792 Uniform Militia Act, all men ages 18–45 were part of the "unorganized militia."	The 1792 Uniform Militia Act was amended twice during the Civil War. The authority to call on the militia was based on Article 1, Section 8's provisions to suppress insurrection. With the March 1863 Enrollment Act, volunteers (and draftees) were brought into federal service under the "raise and support armies" clause.	After organizing volunteer regiments and, in some cases, providing initial training, states sent them to rendezvous points where the regiments were brought into federal service and assigned to higher brigades for service in the various theaters of war. Terms of service ranged from 6 months to 3 years to the full duration of the war.	The Civil War. Although the states produced these kinds of volunteer units for the Mexican-American War and, in a more limited sense, the War of 1812, the aggregate size of the Union Army, made up largely of volunteer regiments, makes the Civil War distinct from previous U.S. wars.	None.
Federal volunteers for the Spanish-American War	The 1898 Volunteer Army Act authorized the federal government to organize, directly, volunteers with "special qualifications." As a result, three federal cavalry regiments were raised (one of which was Leonard Wood's and Teddy Roosevelt's 1st Volunteer Cavalry). These regiments were formed in territories rather than states to encourage volunteerism beyond state political limitations.	The 1898 Volunteer Army Act stipulated that these federal volunteer cavalry regiments would be organized in the territories directly by the federal government under the Constitution's armies clause. They were intentionally formed in the territories to bypass problems with the individual states and their governors, who were forming militia units for volunteering into federal service.	Only one volunteer cavalry regiment was actually formed: Wood and Roosevelt's 1st Volunteer Cavalry, which deployed with Regular Army forces to Cuba, was brigaded with a Regular Army cavalry division, and fought heroically at the Battle of San Juan Hill.	The Spanish-American War from April to August 1898. They were formed using existing territorial militia companies and individual volunteers in the territories of Arizona, New Mexico, and Oklahoma, as well as volunteers from across the nation, and consolidated their training in San Antonio, Texas. Men from the northeast who were friends of Roosevelt also volunteered as enlisted men and officers.	None.

APPENDIX B

Summary Table of Legislation Pertaining to the Evolution of U.S. Military Policy

Table B.1
Summary Table of Legislation Pertaining to the Evolution of U.S. Military Policy

Statute/Act	Historical Context	Significance	Links to Titles 10 and 32
U.S. Constitution: Militia, Raise/ Support Armies, and President as Commander in Chief Clauses	• 1787: Framers want small standing army • Framers envision a select portion of the militia as a federal reserve • Framers also envision the militia as the military force to deal with domestic issues such as insurrection and enforcement of laws	• The constitutional basis for Regular Army, federal army reserve, and militias • No constitutional link between Regular Army and militia • Future policy—laws enacted—would therefore define roles of militia and Regular Army	• Title 32 states National Guard is trained and has its officers appointed under militia clause • Title 10 organized current U.S. Army under raise/ support armies clause
1792 Uniform Militia Act	• George Washington wants militia organized on his 1783 "Sentiments on a Peace Establishment"	• Congress passes militia law with no mechanism for federal enforcement • Is based on militia clause of Constitution • Only militia law until 1903	• Title 32 acknowledges 1792 act and that National Guard is organized under the militia clauses of the Constitution
1795 Amendment to the 1792 Calling Forth Act	• Concern over 1794 Whiskey Rebellion and possible future rebellions • Congress's trust in Washington allows them to give Executive control over militia to deal with domestic problems	• Gives President power to call forth militia without restrictions placed by the 1792 act • Starts the statutory movement away from the militia envisioned in Constitution	• Title 10 gives president authority to either "call forth" or "order" National Guard without congressional authorization per 1795 act
1799 "Augment the Army" Act	• Failure of negotiations with France increased fear of war between the two nations • Domestic unrest at home over taxes to pay for military mobilization increases need for expanded military to deal with insurrections	• Gives President power to expand temporarily the Regular Army by 24 regiments • President given authority to accept organized companies of volunteers from the militia into federal service • 1799 act gives President authority to use this expanded Army for the same purposes when "calling forth" the militia	• Title 10 gives President power to expand Regular Army and use it for domestic problems in combination with National Guard per the 1795 act

Table B.1—continued

Statute/Act	Historical Context	Significance	Links to Titles 10 and 32
1807 Insurrection Act	• With frontier expanding and continuing domestic unrest, there is need for Regular Army for internal problems in addition to Militias	• Gives President authority to use the Regular Army and Navy for internal rebellions and other problems • Completes the statutory movement away from militia envisioned in Constitution	• Title 10 gives President authority to use Regular forces for domestic problems
1863 Enrollment Act	• American Civil War. Union Army having trouble relying on states to bring men and units under federal control to meet manpower demand after two years of war with high casualties	• First federal statutory law that authorized a federal draft premised on universal military duty under the "raise and support armies" clause	• Title 10 relies on the Constitution to give it the statutory means to raise and support an army • Implicit is the assumption that a national draft might be necessary to do so, as stipulated in Title 50
1898 Act to Provide for Temporarily Increasing the Peace Establishment of the United States in Time of War	• Spanish-American War. Regular Army and state National Guards largely unprepared for expeditionary warfare • Debacle of deploying the Army to Cuba to fight Spain spurs significant postwar Army reforms	• Continues Congress on path increasing reliance on armies clause to organize army for war and maintains precedent for American men liable for service in "national forces"	• Same as 1863 Enrollment Act
1903 Act to Promote Efficiency of Militia (Dick Act)	• Spanish-American War reveals problems expanding Army and its readiness • Secretary of War (Elihu Root) implements major reforms for U.S. Army • United States enters world stage as new global power • Perceived need for major Army reform to fight 20th century industrial wars	• First update to Uniform Militia Act for federal organizing of militia since 1792 • Is based on militia clause • Is statutory birthday of modern Guard • Federal government recognizes state Guards as "organized militia" • Directs state Guards to be organized like Regular Army • Establishes federal oversight • Formalizes process of trading autonomy for federal aid • Directs Guard units to train for a minimum of 24 drill periods per year, including a 5-day summer encampment • Funds Guard 5-day encampments	• Title 32 refers to Guard as "organized militia" and directs state Guards to be organized like Regular Army • Title 32 is premised on militia clause and armies clause of Constitution

Table B.1—continued

Statute/Act	Historical Context	Significance	Links to Titles 10 and 32
1908 Army Medical Department Act (April)	• Experience In Spanish-American War with casualties because of poor sanitation and health issues drives need for reform in Army medical care	• Establishes Medical Reserve Corps • Statutory birthday of Army Reserve	• Title 10 Army Reserve premised on armies clause
1908 Dick Act Amendment	• Growing tension between Regular Army and War Department and state Guards • Constitutional debate over use of state Guards in foreign wars as organized militia • State Guards worry federal volunteers will eclipse their desire to be in first line of defense	• Establishes state National Guards as Organized Militia of Several States when called to federal service before any volunteers (individuals or units) and can deploy overseas • Further stokes legal debate over constitutionality of deploying the state Guards, organized on the militia clause, outside of United States	• Title 32 stipulates state Guards are trained and have their officers appointed under the militia clause
1916 National Defense Act	• World War I underway for two years • Mexican border issues • Debate over whether to have federal-only reserve or state National Guards as reserve in first line of defense • Need to reorganize Army for industrial-age warfare • Preparedness movement led by Elihu Root and other leading progressives argues for centralization of Army, universal military training for all American adult males, and rejection of state Guards as reserve force to Army, calls for federal reserve force envisioned in the War Department's "Continental Army Plan"	• Establishes National Guard as component of Army when federalized and in service of the United States • Constitutional premise is armies clause • Directs state Guards to be organized like Regular Army • Gives detailed organization direction for Army • Establishes Organized Reserves and Reserve Officers' Training Corps (ROTC) • Funds Guard for weekly armory training • Is major increase of federal oversight and control of Guard • Sets end strength goal for state Guards at 435,000 and Regular Army at 280,000 • States that Guards when federalized will be drafted as individuals • Establishes Militia Bureau under Secretary of War, not Army Chief of Staff	• Title 10 recognizes the Army National Guard of the United States as a standing reserve component of the Army • Virtually all funding for National Guard under Title 10 is based on Congress organizing the Guard for war under the armies clause • Title 10 allows for Reserve Officers Training

Table B.1—continued

Statute/Act	Historical Context	Significance	Links to Titles 10 and 32
1917 Selective Service Act	• U.S. enters World War I, needs to form quickly a mass citizen-based war army • Selective Service national draft is the means to provide manpower	• First major national draft in American history • Draws on 1898 act and 1863 Enrollment Act that virtually all adult males are susceptible to federal military service • First time Army receives major amounts of manpower without using the state militia systems	• Title 10 is statutory framework to carry out constitutional provision to raise and support armies • National conscription is an implicit mechanism in Title 10 and explicitly stated in Title 50, to carry out that function, if needed • Conscription into federal forces premised on armies clause
1920 Army Reorganization Act (amendment to 1916 National Defense Act)	• End of World War I yields more debate on how to organize peacetime army • War Department produces plan similar to 1915 Continental Army Plan that calls for federal-only reserve to Army • Backlash from Congress • John M. Palmer becomes key adviser to Senate Military Affairs Committee • Demobilization of Guard as individuals not units embitters Guard toward Regular Army	• Continues much of 1916 National Defense Act • Sets end strength goal for Guard 435,000, Regular Army 280,000 (but over next 20 years neither is funded to those levels) • Word "draft" used to bring Guard to federal service but says Guard can be used for any mission (implying foreign wars) • Makes Chief of Militia a Guard officer (formerly a Regular Army officer); also says if Guard demobilized from federal service will be by units, not individuals	• Title 10 National Guard Bureau headed by Guard officer
1933 National Guard Act (amendment to 1916 National Defense Act)	• Main problem is how to mobilize mass citizen-based war army • Both Regular Army and Guard at 50% • Organized Reserve units are manned at skeleton levels • Based on World War I experience, National Guard Association of the United States and Guard lobby Congress hard for Guard to be made reserve component of Army at all times. • National Guard had sought this kind of legislation since the years following end of World War I	• Is statutory birth of modern guard as dual state and federal reserve force • Establishes U.S. Army as the Regular Army, the National Guard of the United States, the National Guard while in the service of the United States, the Officers Reserve Corps, the Organized Reserves, and the Enlisted Reserve Corps • Says Guard is reserve component of U.S. Army at all times; because Guard is permanent reserve of Army the word "ordered" is used for first time • The statutory birthday of the modern Army Total Force	• Title 10 defines U.S. Army as Regular Army, Army National Guard of the Several States, the Army National Guard while in the Service of the United States, and the Army Reserve • Title 10 uses "call forth" and "order" to federalize Guard • Joins the armies and militia clauses into statutory law. • Title 32 reflects "joining" by stating Guard is trained and has officers appointed under militia clause; however, it is organized and equipped under the armies clause

Table B.1—continued

Statute/Act	Historical Context	Significance	Links to Titles 10 and 32
1940 Selective Service Act	• World War II looms • Regular Army, Guard, and Organized Reserves mobilizing and preparing • Palmer brought back by Marshall to think about postwar military policy • Guard worries again about being eclipsed by War Department relying on Army Reserve before Guard	• Stipulates explicitly the term "traditional military policy of the United States" is to maintain "at all times" the National Guard as "integral part of first line defenses"	• Title 32 (as does Title 50) stipulates almost verbatim the term "traditional military policy" as stated in the 1940 Selective Service Act

APPENDIX C

Taxonomy of Important Terms

Active component: This term is often used as a substitute for the Regular component of any of the military Services, and is often confused with *active duty.*

Active duty: The term *active duty* means full-time duty in the active military service of the United States. The term includes full-time training duty, annual training duty, and attendance, while in the active military service, at a school designated as a service school by law or by the Secretary of the military department concerned. The term does not include full-time National Guard duty (10 USC 101(d)(1)).

Armies clause: Article I, Section 8, of the U.S. Constitution states that Congress "shall have the power to," among other things, "raise and support Armies, but no Appropriation of Money to that Use shall be for a longer Term than Two Years."

Army National Guard (ARNG): ARNG is defined in 32 USC 101 as "that part of the organized militia of the several States and Territories, Puerto Rico, and the District of Columbia, active and inactive that a) is a land force; b) is trained, and has its officers appointed, under the 16th clause of section 8, article I, of the Constitution; c) is organized, armed, and equipped wholly or partly at Federal expense; and d) is federally recognized." The National Defense Act of 1916 introduced the use of the term *National Guard* for the organized militia. After the National Security Act of 1947 created the Air Force, the term *Army National Guard* was established to distinguish the land force. When referring to the Army National Guard as a reserve component of the Army, either of the terms *reserve component* (singular) or *reserve components* (plural) should be used. Title 10 of the U.S. Code generally uses the plural term, but it also uses the singular term, which is why either of the two can be used. See also *Army National Guard of the United States* and *National Guard.*

Army National Guard of the United States (ARNGUS): The ARNGUS is the reserve component of the Army all of whose members are members of the Army National Guard (10 USC 101(c)(3)). See also *Army National Guard* and *National Guard.*

Army of the United States divisions, World War II: Formed by the War Department starting in 1943, these were divisions formed in excess to what the 1920 Amendment had established: 9 Regular Army, 18 National Guard, and 36 Organized Reserve divisions.

Army Total Force Policy: This is a formal term adopted in DoD and Department of the Army policy (not statutory law) documents starting in 1970 with Secretary of Defense Melvin Laird's "Total Force Policy" for the entire DoD. It would be incorrect to apply this term to the U.S. Army of 1936, or even 1966, since it is a specific historical term that emerged in a specific historical context. This term was created in an attempt to characterize a shift in DoD thinking, which included higher expectations for the annual investments made in reserve forces and resulting higher levels of readiness.

Calling forth militia clause: Article 1, Section 8, of the U.S. Constitution states that Congress "shall have the power to," among other things, "provide for calling forth The militia to execute the Laws of the Union, suppress Insurrections and repel Invasions."

Chief of the National Guard Bureau (CNGB): The Chief of the National Guard Bureau is responsible for the organization and operation of the National Guard Bureau but does not exercise command over the Army and Air National Guards of the States and Territories. The CNGB serves as a principal adviser to the Secretary of Defense, the Chairman of the Joint Chiefs of Staff, and the Secretaries and Service Chiefs of the Army and Air Force on issues related to the nonfederalized National Guard. In 2011, Congress revised 10 USC 10502 to include the CNGB as a four-star general and as a member of the Joint Chiefs of Staff.

Commander-in-chief clause: Article II, Section 2, of the U.S. Constitution states that "The President shall be Commander in Chief of the Army and Navy of the United States, and of the Militia of the several States, when called into the actual service of the United States . . ."

Director of the Army National Guard (DARNG): Since 1948 and under 10 USC 10506, the DARNG is appointed by the President and is tasked with assisting the Chief of the National Guard Bureau in carrying out the functions of the National Guard Bureau related to the Army National Guard. To be eligible for this four-year post, the officer must be an active member of the Army National Guard and have been nominated for selection by his or her governor or, in the case of the District of Columbia, the commanding general of the District of Columbia National Guard. The president may, with or without the Secretary of Defense's recommendation, appoint the DARNG from general officers of the Army National Guard.

Enlisted Reserve Corps (ERC): Established in federal law by the 1916 National Defense Act, the ERC comprised prior enlisted men from the Regular Army and new enlistees who would receive specialty skills training in the Regular Army. It was similar to the Officers Reserve Corps in that it was intended to provide a manpower replacement pool of enlisted soldiers with special skills for Engineers, Signal, Quartermaster, and Medical Corps to expand the Regular Army when needed. But, like the Officers Reserve Corps, the law allowed the President to assign ERC members as reservists to the Regular Army or to form new reserve organizations. Only a handful of men came into the ERC.

First-line defenses and **second-line defenses:** *First-line defenses* refers to U.S. ground and naval forces that will first meet an enemy of the United States in combat. *Second-line defenses* refers to follow-on forces that will take much longer to mobilize and prepare for battle. For example, in the 19th century, the first line of ground defenses against an invasion from a foreign power was the small Regular Army scattered throughout the country alongside the state militias. The second line in this context would have been a larger volunteer army that would be mobilized by the several states and provided for federal service. In the 20th century, which ground forces were in the first and second lines of defense became the subject of debate among the War Department, Regular Army, and National Guard proponents. Guardsmen saw their organized state militia units as being a part of the first-line defense with the Regular Army. In their view, the Regular Army would respond first but would be quickly joined by ready National Guard units. In this view, the second line would have been the larger volunteer or conscript army. Many Regular Army officers contested this view, arguing that the first-line defenses ought to comprise only the Regular Army and a federal reserve force. The second line of defense, in their view, would have been the larger militia and volunteer army that would take time to mobilize and train. In this view, the state National Guards would be dedicated to state missions, and not typically part of the larger war army, which many Regular Army officers believed must be under the command of one commander-in-chief, namely the President, and not subordinate to state governors, as were the state National Guards.

Inactive Duty for Training (IDT): First codified in 1952, this term refers to authorized training performed by a member of the Army Reserve or National Guard not on active duty or active duty for training. Commonly known as "weekend drill," IDT includes regularly scheduled unit training assemblies, equivalent or additional training, and any special duties authorized for reserve component personnel by the Secretary concerned.

Medical Reserve Corps: Established in federal law on April 23, 1908, in response to capability shortfalls during the 1898 Spanish-American War, the Medical Reserve Corps was the first federal reserve to the U.S. Army organized under the armies clause.

It was to be made up of certified medical doctors who had volunteered to serve in the Medical Reserve Corps and be called to active service when the need was determined by the Secretary of War. This Medical Reserve Corps was the forerunner of the modern Army Reserve of today.

Military policy: Refers to the foundational laws that govern the U.S. Army by defining what the Army consists of—its component parts—and the relationship between those component parts. The first true legal statement of a military policy to govern the Army was the 1916 National Defense Act, although that law did not use the term explicitly. See also *traditional military policy.*

Militia: See Appendix A: Summary Table of 19th Century Militias and Volunteer Forces. Also see *organized militia.*

Militia clause: Article 1, Section 8, of the U.S. Constitution states that Congress "shall have the power to," among other things, "provide for organizing, arming, and disciplining, the Militia, and for governing such Part of them as may be employed in the Service of the United States, reserving to the States respectively, the Appointment of the Officers, and the Authority of training the Militia according to the discipline prescribed by Congress."

Mobilize or mobilization: Refers to either calling forth militias of the several states or ordering the reserve components to federal service to augment the Regular Army.

National Army divisions, World War I: Established by the War Department in 1917 to designate newly formed Army divisions that were made up of draftees (and cadres from Regular Army and National Guard formations) that were created in addition to Regular Army and National Guard divisions.

National Guard: The National Guard evolved out of the volunteer uniformed militias that developed prior to the Civil War. After the Civil War, starting in the 1870s, volunteer uniformed militia units increasingly called themselves National Guard or National Guards. Until the early 20th century, these National Guard units were state entities unto themselves with little or no federal oversight or authority. With the Dick Act in 1903 came federal recognition of the National Guard units as the "organized militia" of the several states. Over the course of the 20th century, the level of federal funding for the National Guard increased to the point that, today, virtually all of the funding for the National Guard comes from the federal government. See also *Army National Guard* and *Army National Guard of the United States.*

Officers' Reserve Corps: Established in federal law by the 1916 National Defense Act to facilitate the rapid expansion of the Army, the Officers' Reserve Corps was to consist of men who had volunteered to be in it, had received the appropriate level of training as further stipulated by the 1916 act, and would be liable to be ordered by the President to federal service to fill out and expand the ranks of the Regular Army. The Officers' Reserve Corps was premised on the armies clause. Its historical use was generally during the period between 1916 and 1941.

Organized militia and **unorganized militia:** The first use of the term *organized militia* in federal law was in the 1903 Dick Act, which recognized the National Guards of the several states as the "organized militia" and premised on the militia clauses. This statutory term should not be confused with various militia units in 18th and 19th century America that were organized, either under compulsory service or volunteerism.

The term *unorganized militia* was first stipulated in federal law in the 1903 Dick Act to refer to men between ages 18 and 45 who were not members of the state National Guards or "organized militia."

Organized Reserve Corps: This term is often used in post–World War II writings to describe the "Organized Reserves" during the interwar years from 1920 to 1940. The term *Organized Reserve Corps* was not used during those interwar years unless someone was referring to an actual "corps" formation in the Organized Reserves. The term *Organized Reserve Corps* came into use during the World War II years, especially when planners were writing about postwar Army organizations. However, the term was first stipulated in federal law in the Army Organization Act of 1950. The 1952 Armed Forces Reserve Act then stipulated the term *Organized Reserve Corps* would be replaced with *Army Reserve*. Therefore, the term *Organized Reserve Corps* should be used carefully and only when referring to the years between roughly 1944 and 1952. Unfortunately, many secondary sources use *Organized Reserve Corps* interchangeably with *Organized Reserves* to describe the Organized Reserves during the interwar years. One other point of confusion is that the abbreviation *ORC* is also used for the Officers Reserve Corps; the two organizations are obviously quite different and distinct.

Organized Reserves: Established in the 1920 amendment to the 1916 National Defense Act, the Organized Reserves consisted of the Officers Reserve Corps and the Enlisted Reserve Corps. The 1920 law added this new term from the 1916 National Defense Act for organizational purposes, because when World War I ended in 1918, the Department of War intended to maintain in peacetime an organized Army reserve, under the armies clause, that had actual "in being" corps, divisions, regiments, etc. A big difference from the National Guard was that the Organized Reserve units were of skeletal strength, consisting only of officers. Importantly, the 1920 amendment designated nine corps regional areas in the United States responsible for training and recruiting for the Regular Army, National Guard, and Organized Reserve divisions in it. The 1920 amendment stipulated that each corps area would have one Regular Army division, two National Guard divisions, and three Organized Reserve divisions.

This force structure would become the nucleus for a greater Army expansion in World War II.

Regular Army: In continuous existence since 1788 as stipulated in federal law, the Regular Army is the full-time, standing component of the Army. The term *active duty* is often used as being synonymous with the Regular Army, but it is not. The confusion comes from the premise of the Regular Army being a full-time "active" force.

Reserve component: This singular term may refer to any of the reserve components of the military services or the Coast Guard described below under *reserve components*. With regard to the Army, *reserve component* may refer to either the Army Reserve or the Army National Guard of the United States. The term first appeared in the Code of Federal Regulations in 1926, when Title 32 defined the National Guard as the United States' reserve component. It has since expanded in line with the emergence of additional reserve forces.

Reserve components: As codified in 1994 in 10 USC 10101, *reserve components* is the collective term for the seven individual reserve components of the U.S. military: Army National Guard of the United States, Army Reserve, Marine Corps Force Reserve, Navy Reserve, Air National Guard of the United States, Air Force Reserve, and Coast Guard Reserve. Under 10 USC 10102, the purpose of the reserve components is to "provide trained units and qualified persons available for active duty in the armed forces, in time of war or national emergency, and at such other times as the national security may require, to fill the needs of the armed forces whenever more units and persons are needed than are in the regular components."

Reserve Officers' Training Corps (ROTC): The ROTC was established in statutory law by the 1916 National Defense Act. The law authorized the President, under the armies clause, to establish ROTC detachments at U.S. colleges granting four-year degrees. The law also mandated ROTC detachments at U.S. colleges and universities that were established by the 1862 U.S. land grant (Morrell Act), which provided federal land to newly formed states to build colleges and universities. A provision of the Morrell Act directed that military tactics and sciences be taught at these land grant institutions. Hence the connection between the 1916 National Defense Act establishing the ROTC and the 1862 Morrell Act.

Traditional military policy: A term created by an important Army reformer of the first half of the 20th century, John McAuley Palmer. Palmer first used the term in a report he wrote for the Secretary of War Henry Stimson in 1912. In Palmer's view, the "traditional military policy" of the United States was to have a small Regular Army in peacetime that would be expanded by mobilizing the mass of the citizenry into a war army that was also led by "citizen soldiers." Palmer also began in the years prior to World War I to add an additional tenet of this "traditional military policy," which was to have this citizen army in place in peacetime so that it could be equipped and trained. In 1940, Congress applied the term *traditional military policy* in statutory law to the National Guard, by stating "in accordance with the traditional military policy of the United States, it is essential that the strength and organization of the National Guard as an integral part of the first line defenses of the United States be maintained and assured at all times . . ."

U.S. Army or **Army:** The term *Army* refers to the totality of the U.S. Army at any given time in U.S. history—that is, the Regular Army and whatever type of force has been added to expand it. It is incorrect to assume that the term *Army* is synonymous with *Regular Army*; *Army* refers to the Regular Army *and* the actual or potential means to expand it. For example, one could use the term *Army* during the War of 1812 to mean the Regular Army, compulsory militia units provided by the several states to expand the overall size of the Army, and volunteer militia units from the several states. Or, by way of another example, the term *Army* in 1944 meant units of the Regular Army, Organized Reserves, the National Guards of the states and territories, and the Army of the United States. As a more recent example, the term *Army*, as stipulated in Title 10 of the U.S. Code, means the Regular Army, the Army National Guard of the United States, the Army National Guard while in the service of the United States, and the Army Reserve (i.e., the U.S. Army Reserve). The Army recognizes its birthday as occurring in 1775, when the Continental Congress established the American "Continental" Army.

U.S. Army Reserve: The 1952 Armed Forces Reserve Act, a major piece of legislation reforming all of the military services' reserve components, largely based on the experience of the partial mobilization during the Korean War, replaced older terms for the Army, such as *Organized Reserves* and *Organized Reserve Corps* with the new term *Army Reserve.* It is important to note that this legal title should be used in singular form and not in the plural—*Army Reserves*—since in its singular form, as stipulated in law, it refers to the individual members and units of the Army Reserve. At the Department of Defense (DoD) level, it is typical to refer to the *reserves* (plural and lowercase) when referring collectively to the Army Reserve, Navy Reserve, Air Force Reserve, Marine Corps Forces Reserve, and Coast Guard Reserve—but, importantly, not the Army National Guard. When referring to the Army Reserve as a reserve component of the Army, the term *reserve component* should be used; the *Army reserve components* are the U.S. Army Reserve and the Army National Guard of the United States.

References

Adams, Willi Paul, *The First American Constitutions: Republican Ideology and the Making of the State Constitutions in the Revolutionary Era*, Chapel Hill, N.C.: Published for the Institute of Early American History and Culture, Williamsburg, Virginia, by the University of North Carolina Press, 1980.

Ambrose, Stephen E., *Upton and the Army*, Baton Rouge, La.: Louisiana State University Press, (1964) 1993.

Ames, H. V., ed., *State Documents on Federal Relations: The States and the United States*, Philadelphia, Pa.: University of Pennsylvania, 1911.

"An Act Providing for the Prosecution of the Existing War Between the United States and the Republic of Mexico (Approved May 13, 1846)," in John F. Callan, ed., *The Military Laws of the United States*, Philadelphia, Pa.: George W. Childs, 1863.

Anderson, Fred, *A People's Army: Massachusetts Soldiers and Society in the Seven Years' War*, Chapel Hill, N.C.: University of North Carolina Press, 1984.

———, *Crucible of War: The Seven Years' War and the Fate of Empire in British North America, 1754–1766*, New York: Alfred A. Knopf, 2000.

Anonymous, "The Federalist Farmer No. XVIII" (1788), in Herbert J. Storing, ed., *The Complete Anti-Federalist*, Chicago, Ill.: University of Chicago Press, 1981, pp. 339–349.

Babits, Lawrence E., *A Devil of a Whipping: The Battle of Cowpens*, Chapel Hill, N.C.: University of North Carolina Press, 1998.

Bacevich, Andrew, "Emory Upton: A Centennial Assessment," *Military Review*, December 1981.

Bahar, Michael, "The Presidential Intervention Principle: The Domestic Use of the Military and the Power of the Several States," *Harvard National Security Journal*, Vol. 5, 2014.

Bailey, Kenneth Roy, *A Search for Identity: The West Virginia National Guard, 1877–1921*, dissertation, Ohio State University, 1976.

Bancroft, Frederic, *Calhoun and the South Carolina Nullification Movement*, Baltimore, Md.: Johns Hopkins University Press, 1967.

Barron, David J., and Martin S. Ledermen, "The Commander in Chief at the Lowest Ebb: A Constitutional History," *Harvard Law Review*, Vol. 1, No. 4, February 2008.

Barry, Richard, "Emory Upton, Military Genius—Practically Unknown General, for Whom Camp at Yaphank Was Named, Advocated Many Years Ago Reforms Embodied in Our Great Army of Today," *New York Times*, June 16, 1918.

Bauer, K. Jack, "The Battles on the Rio Grande: Palo Alto and Resaca de la Palma, 8–9 May 1846," in William Stoft and Charles Heller, eds., *1776–1965, America's First Battles*, Lawrence, Kans.: Kansas University Press, 1984.

Bauer, K. Jack, and H. Sutton James, Jr., *The Mexican War, 1846–1848*, New York: Macmillan, 1974.

Beckett, I. F. W., *Britain's Part-Time Soldiers: The Amateur Military Tradition 1558–1945*, Barnsley, UK: Pen & Sword Military, 2011.

Bernstein, Iver, *The New York City Draft Riots: Their Significance for American Society and Politics in the Age of the Civil War*, New York: Oxford University Press, 1990.

Bixby, William K., *Letters of Zachary Taylor from the Battlefield of the Mexican War*, Rochester, N.Y.: The Post Express Printing Co., 1908.

Boies, Henry Martyn, "Our National Guard," *Harper's New Monthly Magazine*, 1880, pp. 915–922.

Borneman, Walter R., *1812: The War that Forged a Nation*, New York: Harper Perennial, 2004.

Bouton, Terry, *Taming Democracy: "The People," the Founders, and the Troubled Ending of the American Revolution*, New York: Oxford University Press, 2007.

Boyd, Steven R., ed., *The Whiskey Rebellion: Past and Present Perspectives*, Westport, Conn.: Greenwood Press, 1985.

"A Brief History of the Oldest Minnesota National Guard Company," *National Guardsman*, May 1901.

Brooks, Charles B., *The Siege of New Orleans*, Seattle, Wash.: University of Washington Press, 1961.

Brown, Richard C., "General Emory Upton—The Army's Mahan," *Military Affairs*, Vol. 17, No. 3, 1953, pp. 125–131.

Calhoun, John C., *Report of the Secretary of War of a Plan for the Reduction of the Army of the United States (December 12, 1820)*, Referred to the Committee on Military Affairs, Washington, D.C.: Gales & Seaton, 1820.

Carney, Stephen A., *Guns Along the Rio Grande: Palo Alto and Resaca de la Palma*, Washington, D.C.: U.S. Army Center of Military History, 2005.

Cheseldine, R. M., "Where Emory Upton Made His Big Mistake," *Infantry Journal*, March 1930.

Cirillo, Vincent J., *Bullets and Bacilli: The Spanish-American War and Military Medicine*, New Brunswick, N.J.: Rutgers University Press, 2004.

Clark, J. P., *Preparing for War: The Emergence of the Modern U.S. Army, 1815–1917*, Cambridge, Mass.: Harvard University Press, 2017.

Clary, David A., and Joseph W. A. Whitehorne, *The Inspectors General of the United States Army, 1777–1903*, Washington, D.C.: U.S, Army Center of Military History, 1987.

Coakley, Robert, *Federal Use of Militia and the National Guard in Civil Disturbances*, Washington, D.C: Brookings Institution, 1941.

———, *The Role of Federal Military Forces in Domestic Disorders, 1789–1878*, Washington, D.C.: U.S. Army Center of Military History, 1989.

Coffman, Edward M., *The Old Army: A Portrait of the American Army in Peacetime, 1784–1898*, New York: Oxford University Press, 1986.

Cohen, Eliot, *Making Do With Less, or Coping with Emory Upton's Ghost*, Carlisle Barracks, Pa.: U.S. Army War College, 1995.

Congressional Record, Annals of Congress, 2nd Congress, 1st Session, February 21, 1792a.

Congressional Record, Annals of Congress, 2nd Congress, 2nd Session, April 23, 1792b.

Congressional Record, Annals of Congress, 3rd Congress, 1st Session, May 30, 1794.

Congressional Record, Annals of Congress, 3rd Congress, 2nd Session, February 12, 1795.

Cooper, Jerry, "National Guard Reform, The Army, and the Spanish-American War: The View from Wisconsin," *Military Affairs*, Vol. 42, No. 1, January 1978.

———, *The Militia and National Guard in America Since Colonial Times: A Reference Guide*, Westport, Conn.: Greenwood Press, 1993.

Cooper, Jerry M., *The Rise of the National Guard: The Evolution of the American Militia, 1865–1920*, Lincoln, Neb.: University of Nebraska Press, 1998.

Cosmas, Graham A., "From Order to Chaos: The War Department, the National Guard, and Military Policy, 1898," *Military Affairs*, Vol. 29, No. 3, Autumn 1965.

———, *An Army for Empire: The United States Army in the Spanish-American War*, College Station, Tex.: Texas A&M University Press, 1998.

Coulter, E. Merton, and Frank L. Owsley, "The Confederate States of America, 1861–1865," *The Journal of Economic History*, Vol. 10, No. 2, 1950, pp. 230–231.

Cunliffe, Marcus, *Soldiers and Civilians: The Martial Spirit in America, 1775–1865*, Boston, Mass.: Little, Brown, 1968.

Currie, David P., *The Constitution in Congress: The Federalist Period 1789–1801*, Chicago, Ill.: University of Chicago Press, 1997.

Davis, Burke, *The Cowpens-Guilford Courthouse Campaign*, Philadelphia, Pa.: University of Pennsylvania Press, 2002.

Derthick, Martha, *The National Guard in Politics*, Cambridge, Mass.: Harvard University Press, 1965.

Doubler, Michael D., *I Am the Guard: A History of the Army National Guard, 1636–2000*, Washington, D.C.: Army National Guard, 2001.

Drake, James David, *King Philip's War: Civil War in New England, 1675–1676*, Amherst, Mass.: University of Massachusetts Press, 1999.

Duggan, Joseph Charles, *The Legislative and Statutory Development of the Federal Concept of Conscription for Military Service*, Washington, D.C.: Catholic University of America Press, 1946.

Eisenhower, John S. D., *So Far from God: The U.S. War with Mexico, 1846–1848*, Norman, Okla.: University of Oklahoma Press, 2000.

Engdahl, David E., "Soldiers, Riots, and Revolutions: The Law and History of Military Troops in Civil Disorders," *Iowa Law Review*, Vol. 57, No. 1, October 1971.

Farrand, M., "The Delaware Bill of Rights of 1776," *The American Historical Review*, Vol. 3, 1898.

Fitzpatrick, David, *Emory Upton: The Misunderstood Reformer*, PhD dissertation, Ann Arbor, Mich.: University of Michigan, 1996.

———, "Emory Upton and the Citizen Soldier," *Journal of Military History*, April 2001.

Foner, Jack D., *The United States Soldier Between Two Wars: Army Life and Reforms, 1865–1898*, New York: Humanities Press, 1970.

Frederick, Todd P., "Our National Guard: An Introduction to Its History," *Military Affairs*, Vol. 5, No. 3, 1941.

Friedman, Leon, "Conscription and the Constitution: The Original Understanding," *Michigan Law Review*, Vol. 67, May 1969, pp. 1493–1552.

Gaff, Allan D., *Bayonets in the Wilderness: Anthony Wayne's Legion in the Old Northwest*, Norman, Okla.: University of Oklahoma Press, 2004.

Galloway, Eilene Marie Slack, *History of United States Military Policy on Reserve Forces, 1775–1957*, Washington, D.C.: U.S. Government Printing Office, 1957.

Geary, James W., *We Need Men: The Union Draft in the Civil War*, DeKalb, Ill.: Northern Illinois University Press, 1991.

Glatthaar, Joseph T., *General Lee's Army: From Victory to Collapse*, New York: Free Press, 2008.

Goodman, David, *Gold Seeking: Victoria and California in the 1850s*, Stanford, Calif.: Stanford University Press, 1994.

Grant, Ulysses S., *Personal Memoirs*, New York: The Modern Library, 1885.

Gross, Robert A., "A Yankee Rebellion? The Regulators, New England, and the New Nation," *New England Quarterly*, Vol. 82, No. 1, March 2009, pp. 112–135.

Grove, John G., *John C. Calhoun's Theory of Republicanism*, Lawrence, Kans.: University Press of Kansas, 2016.

Hadden, Sally E., *Slave Patrols: Law and Violence in Virginia and the Carolinas*, Cambridge, Mass.: Harvard University Press, 2001.

Halleck, H. W., *Report on the Means of National Defence*, Washington, D.C.: Government Printing Office, 1843.

———, *Elements of Military Art and Science; or, Course of Instruction in Strategy, Fortification, Tactics of Battles, &c.; Embracing the Duties of Staff, Infantry, Cavalry, Artillery, and Engineers. Adapted to the Use of Volunteers and Militia*, New York; Philadelphia, Pa.: D. Appleton & Co.; G. S. Appleton, 1846.

Hamilton, Alexander, James Madison, John Jay, and Lawrence Goldman, eds. *The Federalist Papers*, New York: Oxford University Press, 2008.

Harris, William C., *Leroy Pope Walker: Confederate Secretary of War*, Tuscaloosa, Ala.: Confederate Pub. Co., 1962.

Henry, H. M., *The Police Control of the Slave in South Carolina*, Emory, Va., 1914.

Herrera, Ricardo A., *For Liberty and the Republic: The American Citizen as Soldier, 1775–1861*, New York: New York University Press, 2015.

Hesseltine, William Best, *Lincoln and the War Governors*, New York: A. A. Knopf, 1948.

Hice, Jeffrey Neale, *The Utmost Devotion to Duty: Rediscovering the Faith and Character of General Emory Upton*, St. Bonaventure, N.Y.: St. Bonaventure University, 1996.

Hickey, Donald R., *The War of 1812: A Forgotten Conflict*, Urbana, Ill.: University of Illinois Press, 2012.

———, *Glorious Victory: Andrew Jackson and the Battle of New Orleans*, Baltimore, Md.: Johns Hopkins University Press, 2015.

Hill, Jim Dan, *The Minute Man in Peace and War: A History of the National Guard*, Harrisburg, Pa.: Stackpole Books, 1964.

Hirsch, Alan, "The Militia Clause of the Constitution and the National Guard," *University of Cincinnati Law Review*, No. 59, 1988.

History of Congress, "War Measures," October 1814.

Holley, I. B., *General John M. Palmer, Citizen Soldiers, and the Army of a Democracy*, Westport, Conn.: Greenwood Press, 1982.

Holmes, Joseph John, *The National Guard of Pennsylvania: Policeman of Industry, 1865–1905*, PhD dissertation, Storrs, Conn.: University of Connecticut, 1971.

Huntington, Samuel P., *The Soldier and the State: The Theory and Politics of Civil-Military Relations*, Cambridge, Mass.: Belknap Press of Harvard University Press, 1957.

Jackson, Andrew, "Speech to William Pitt Martin and the Citizens of Fayettville, Tennessee (July 5, 1826)," in Harold D. Moser and J. Clint Clifft, eds., *The Papers of Andrew Jackson*: Volume VI: *1825–1828*, Knoxville, Tenn.: University of Tennessee Press, 2002.

Jacobs, James Ripley, *The Beginning of the U.S. Army, 1783–1812*, Princeton, N.J.: Princeton University Press, 1947.

Johannsen, Robert W., *To the Halls of the Montezumas: The Mexican War in the American Imagination*, New York: Oxford University Press, 1988.

Johnson, Timothy, *Winfield Scott: The Quest for Military Glory*, Lawrence, Kans.: University Press of Kansas, 1998.

Jordan, Brian Matthew, *Marching Home: Union Veterans and Their Unending Civil War*, New York: Liveright Publishing Corporation, 2014.

Jordan, William B., *Maine in the Civil War: A Bibliographical Guide*, Portland, Maine: Maine Historical Society, 1976.

Knox, Henry, *A Plan for the General Arrangement of the Militia of the United States*, New York: Francis Childs and John Swaine, 1790.

Kohn, Richard H., "The Washington Administration's Decision to Crush the Whiskey Rebellion," *Journal of American History*, Vol. 59, No. 3, December 1972, pp. 579–582.

———, *Eagle and Sword: Federalists and the Creation of the Military Establishment in America, 1783–1802*, New York: Free Press, 1975.

———, "The Murder of the Militia System in the Aftermath of the American Revolution," in Stanley J. Underdal, ed., *Military History of the American Revolution: The Proceedings of the 6th Military History Symposium of the United States Air Force Academy 10–11 October 1974*, Washington, D.C.: U.S. Government Printing Office, 1976.

———, *The United States Military Under the Constitution of the United States, 1789–1989*, New York: New York University Press, 1991.

Kreidberg, Marvin A., and Merton G. Henry, *History of Military Mobilization in the United States Army, 1775–1945*, Washington, D.C.: Department of the Army, 1955.

Kurtz, Stephen G., "The French Mission of 1799–1800: Concluding Chapter in the Statecraft of John Adams," *Political Science Quarterly*, Vol. 80, No. 4, 1965, pp. 543–557.

Leach, Douglas Edward, *Flintlock and Tomahawk: New England in King Philip's War*, New York: Macmillan, 1958.

Leach, Jack Franklin, *Conscription in the United States: Historical Background*, Rutland, Vt.: C. E. Tuttle Pub. Co., 1952.

Lee, Henry, *The Militia of the United States: What It Has Been, What It Should Be*, Boston, Mass.: Marvin & Son, 1864.

Lerwill, Leonard L., *The Personnel Replacement System in the United States Army*, Washington, D.C.: Department of the Army, 1954.

Levy, Leonard W., *Jefferson & Civil Liberties: The Darker Side*, revised ed., New York: Quadrangle, 1973.

Linn, Brian, *The Echo of Battle: The Army's Way of War*, Cambridge, Mass.: Harvard University Press, 2007.

MacKinnon, William P., *At Sword's Point, Part 1: A Documentary History of the Utah War to 1858*, Norman, Okla.: The Arthur H. Clark Company, 2008.

———, *At Sword's Point, Part 2: A Documentary History of the Utah War, 1858–1859*, Norman, Okla.: University of Oklahoma Press, 2016.

Mahon, John K., *The Citizen Soldier in National Defense, 1789–1815*, PhD dissertation, Los Angeles, Calif.: University of California at Los Angeles, 1950.

———, "A Board of Officers Considers the Condition of the Militia in 1826," *Military Affairs*, Vol. 15, No. 2, Summer 1951.

———, *The American Militia, Decade of Decision, 1789–1800*, Gainesville, Fla.: University Press of Florida, 1960.

———, *History of the Militia and the National Guard*, New York; London: Collier Macmillan, 1983.

———, *History of the Second Seminole War, 1835–1842*, Gainesville, Fla.: University Press of Florida, 2010.

Maier, Pauline, *Ratification: The People Debate the Constitution, 1787–1788*, New York: Simon & Schuster, 2010.

Malbin, Michael J., "Conscription, the Constitution, and the Framers: A Historical Analysis," *Fordham Law Review*, Vol. 40, May 1972, pp. 805–826.

Mansfield, Edward Deering, *The Mexican War: A History of Its Origins*, New York: A. S. Barnes & Co., 1849.

Marcus, Richard Henry, *The Militia of Colonial Connecticut, 1639–1775*, PhD dissertation, Boulder, Colo.: University of Colorado, 1965.

Marszalek, John F., *Commander of All Lincoln's Armies*, Cambridge, Mass.: The Belknap Press of Harvard University Press, 2004.

Marten, James, *Sing Not War: The Lives of Union and Confederate Veterans in Gilded Age America*, Chapel Hill, N.C.: University of North Carolina Press, 2011.

McCaffrey, James M., *Army of Manifest Destiny: The American Soldier in the Mexican War, 1846–1848*, New York: New York University Press, 1992.

McPherson, James M., *Battle Cry of Freedom: The Civil War Era,* New York: Oxford University Press, 1988.

Michie, Peter Smith, and James Harrison Wilson, *The Life and Letters of Emory Upton*, New York: Arno Press, 1979.

Millett, Allan R., Peter Maslowski, and William B. Feis, *For the Common Defense: A Military History of the United States from 1607–2012*, New York: Free Press, 2012.

Millis, Walter, *American Military Thought*, Indianapolis, Ind.: Bobbs-Merrill, 1966.

Moore, Albert Burton, *Conscription and Conflict in the Confederacy*, New York: Macmillan, 1924.

Morrison, James L., Jr., *"The Best School": West Point, 1833–1866*, Kent, Ohio: Kent State University Press, 1998.

Murdock, Eugene C., *Patriotism Limited, 1862–1865: The Civil War Draft and the Bounty System*, Kent, Ohio: Kent State University Press, 1967.

———, *One Million Men: The Civil War Draft in the North*, Madison, Wisc.: State Historical Society of Wisconsin, 1971.

National Commission on the Future of the Army, *Report to the President and the Congress of the United States*, Arlington, Va., January 28, 2016.

Nevins, Allan, *The War for the Union: War Becomes Revolution, 1862–1863*, Volume I, New York: Scribner, 1959.

O'Sullivan, John, and Alan M. Meckler, *The Draft and Its Enemies: A Documentary History*, Champaign, Ill.: University of Illinois Press, 1974.

Palmer, John McAuley, *Report on the Organization of the Land Forces of the United States*, Washington, D.C.: U.S. Department of War, 1912.

———, *America in Arms: The Experience of the United States with Military Organization*, New Haven, Conn.: Yale University Press, 1941.

The Papers of James Madison, Purchased by Order of Congress; Being His Correspondence and Reports of Debates During the Congress of the Confederation and His Reports of Debates in the Federal Convention, Vol. II, New York: J. & H. G. Langley, 1841.

Peskin, Allan, *Winfield Scott and the Profession of Arms,* Kent, Ohio: Kent State University Press, 2003.

Pisney, Raymond F., "The Brandywine Rangers in the War of 1812," Wilmington, Del.: Hagley Museum & Library, 1950.

Pitch, Anthony S., *The Burning of Washington*, Annapolis, Md.: Naval Institute Press, 2000.

Pratt, William D., *A History of the National Guard of Indiana: From the Beginning of the Militia System in 1787 to the Present Time, Including the Services of Indiana Troops in the War with Spain*, Indianapolis, Ind.: W. D. Pratt, Printer and Binder, 1901.

Prucha, Francis Paul, *The Sword of the Republic: The United States Army on the Frontier, 1783–1846*, New York: Macmillan, 1969.

Public Law 113-291, National Defense Authorization Act for Fiscal Year 2015, December 19, 2014.

Quimby, Robert S., *The U.S. Army in the War of 1812: An Operational and Command Study*, East Lansing, Mich.: Michigan State University Press, 1997.

Rakove, Jack N., *Original Meanings: Politics and Ideas in the Making of the Constitution*, New York: A. A. Knopf, 1996.

Rich, Bennett Milton, *The Presidents and Civil Disorder*, Washington, D.C.: Brookings Institution, 1941.

Richards, Leonard L., *Shays' Rebellion: The American Revolution's Final Battle*, Philadelphia:, Pa.: University of Pennsylvania Press, 2002.

Riker, William H., *Soldiers of the States: The Role of the National Guard in American Democracy*, Washington, D.C.: Public Affairs Press, 1957.

Rowland, John Kenneth, *Origins of the Second Amendment: The Creation of the Constitutional Rights of Militia and of Keeping and Bearing Arms*, PhD dissertation, Columbus, Ohio: Ohio State University, 1978.

Schlesinger, Arthur M., Jr., *The Imperial Presidency*, Boston, Mass.: Mariner Books, 2004.

Selesky, Harold E., *War and Society in Colonial Connecticut*, New Haven, Conn.: Yale University Press, 1990.

Shannon, Fred A., *The Organization and Administration of the Union Army*, Bethesda, Md.: University Publications of America, 1994.

Shaw, William L., *The Civil War Federal Conscription and Exemption System*, Washington, D.C.: Judge Advocates Association, 1962a.

———, "The Confederate Conscription and Exemption Acts," *American Journal of Legal History*, Vol. 6, October 1962b, pp. 368–405.

———, "The Interrelationship of the United States Army and the National Guard," *Military Law Review*, No. 39, January 1966, pp. 39–84.

Shea, William L., *The Virginia Militia in the Seventeenth Century*, Baton Rouge, La.: Louisiana State University Press, 1983.

Shy, John, "A New Look at the Colonial Militia," *William and Mary Quarterly*, Vol. 3, No. 20, 1963.

———, "Armed Force in Colonial North America: New Spain, New France, and Anglo-America," in Kenneth J. Hagan and William R. Roberts, eds., *Against All Enemies: Interpretations of American Military History from Colonial Times to the Present*, Westport, Conn.: Greenwood Press, 1986.

Skeen, C. Edward, *Citizen Soldiers in the War of 1812*, Lexington, Ky.: University Press of Kentucky, 1999.

Skelton, William B., *An American Profession of Arms: The Army Officer Corps, 1784–1861*, Lawrence, Kans.: University Press of Kansas, 1992.

Smith, Jonathan, "How Massachusetts Raised Her Troops in the American Revolution," paper presented at Massachusetts Historical Society, January 1922 Meeting: The Plimpton Press, 1922.

Spain, August O., *The Political Theory of John C. Calhoun*, New York: Bookman Associates, 1951.

Sparrow, John C., *History of Personnel Demobilization in the United States Army*, Washington, D.C.: Department of the Army, 1952.

Spiller, Roger, "Calhoun's Expansible Army: The History of a Military Idea," *South Atlantic Quarterly*, No. 79, Spring 1980.

Stagg, J. C. A., *Mr. Madison's War: Politics, Diplomacy, and Warfare in the Early American Republic, 1783–1830*, Princeton, N.J.: Princeton University Press, 1983.

Stewart, Richard W., *American Military History*, Volume I: *The Forging of a Nation, 1775–1917*, Washington, D.C.: U.S. Army Center of Military History, 2009.

———, *American Military History*, Volume II: *The United States Army in a Global Era, 1917–2008*, Washington, D.C.: U.S. Army Center of Military History, 2010.

Stone, Richard G., *A Brittle Sword: The Kentucky Militia, 1776–1912*, Lexington, Ky.: University Press of Kentucky, 2009.

Szatmary, Daniel P., *The Making of an Agrarian Insurrection*, Amherst, Mass.: University of Massachusetts Press, 1980.

Taylor, Alan, *The Civil War of 1812: American Citizens, British Subjects, Irish Rebels, and Indian Allies*, New York: Vintage Books, 2010.

Upton, Emory, *A New System of Infantry Tactics, Double and Single Rank, Adapted to American Topography and Improved Fire-Arms*, New York: D. Appleton, 1868.

———, *The Armies of Asia and Europe: Embracing Official Reports on the Armies of Japan, China, India, Persia, Italy, Russia, Austria, Germany, France, and England*, Portsmouth, England: Griffin & Co., 1878.

———, *The Military Policy of the United States*, 4th ed., Washington, D.C.: U.S. Government Printing Office, 1903.

U.S. Code, Title 32—National Guard, 2012.

U.S. House of Representatives, *Review of the Reserve Program: Hearing Before the Subcommittee No. 1 of the Committee on Armed Services*, Washington, D.C.: U.S. Government Printing Office, February 4–8, 18–21, 1957.

U.S. Senate, Joint Committee on the Reorganization of the Army, *Report to Accompany S.1491*, Washington, D.C.: U.S. Government Printing Office, S. Rep. 555, December 12, 1878.

U.S. Statutes at Large, An Act to Recognize and Adapt to the Constitution of the United States, the Establishment of the Troops Raised Under the Resolve of the United States in Congress Assembled and for Other Purposes Therein Mentioned, First Congress, Sessions I and II, Chapter 25, September 29, 1789.

U.S. Statutes at Large, An Act Providing for Calling Forth the Militia to Execute the Laws of the Union, Suppress Insurrections, and Repel Invasions, Second Congress, Session I, Chapter 28, May 2, 1792a (1 Stat. 264).

U.S. Statutes at Large, An Act to More Effectually to Provide for the National Defense by Establishing a Uniform Militia Throughout the United States, Second Congress, Session I, Chapter 33, May 8, 1792b (1 Stat. 271).

U.S. Statutes at Large, An Act Providing for the Authority for Calling Forth the Militia to Execute the Laws of the Union, Suppress Insurrections, and Repel Invasions; and to Repeal the Act Now in Force for Those Purposes, Third Congress, Session II, Chapter 30, February 28, 1795 (1 Stat. 424).

U.S. Statutes at Large, An Act Giving Eventual Authority to the President of the United States to Augment the Army, Fifth Congress, Session III, Chapter 31, March 2, 1799 (1 Stat. 725).

U.S. Statutes at Large, An Act Authorizing the Employment of the Land and Naval Forces of the United States, in Case of Insurrections, Tenth Congress, Session II, Chapter 39, March 3, 1807 (2 Stat. 443).

U.S. Statutes at Large, An Act to Amend the Act Calling Forth the Militia to Execute the Laws of the Union, Suppress Insurrections, and Repel Invasions, Approved February Twenty-Eight, Seventeen Hundred and Ninety-Five, and the Acts Amendatory Thereof, and for Other Purposes, Thirty-Seventh Congress, Session II, Chapter 201, July 17, 1862 (12 Stat. 597).

U.S. Statutes at Large, An Act for Enrolling and Calling Out the National Forces, and for Other Purposes, Thirty-Seventh Congress, Session III, Chapter 75, March 3, 1863 (12 Stat. 731).

U.S. Statutes at Large, An Act to Amend an Act Entitled "An Act for Enrolling and Calling Out the National Forces, and for Other Purposes," approved March Third, Eighteen Hundred and Sixty-Three, Thirty-Eighth Congress, Session I, Chapter 13, February 24, 1864 (13 Stat. 6).

U.S. Statutes at Large, An Act to Provide for Temporarily Increasing the Military Establishment of the United States in Time of War, and for Other Purposes, Fifty-Fifth Congress, Session II, Chapter 187, April 22, 1898 (30 Stat. 361).

Vladeck, Stephen I., "Emergency Power and the Militia Acts," *The Yale Law Review*, Vol. 114, October 2004.

Wallace, Lew, *Lew Wallace: An Autobiography*, Vol. 1, New York: Harper & Brothers Publishers 1906.

Warren, Jason W., *Connecticut Unscathed: Victory in the Great Narragansett War, 1675–1676*, Norman, Okla.: University of Oklahoma Press, 2014.

Washington, George, "Sentiments on a Peace Establishment" (May 2, 1783), in John C. Fitzpatrick, ed., *The Writings of George Washington from the Original Manuscript Sources, 1745–1799*, Vol. 26, Washington, D.C.: U.S. Government Printing Office, 1938.

Watson, Samuel J., *Jackson's Sword: The Army Officer Corps on the American Frontier, 1810–1821*, Lawrence, Kans.: University Press of Kansas, 2012.

———, *Peacekeepers and Conquerors: The Army Officer Corps on the American Frontier, 1821–1846*, Lawrence, Kans.: University Press of Kansas, 2013.

Webster, Daniel, and John C. Calhoun, *The Constitution Not a Compact Between Sovereign States: A Speech by the Hon. Daniel Webster in the Senate of the United States, Jan., 1833, in Reply to the Resolutions Offered by Mr. Calhoun, of South Carolina, Affirming the Right of Secession*, London: Woodfall and Kinder, 1862.

Weigley, Russell Frank, *Towards an American Army: Military Thought from Washington to Marshall*, New York: Columbia University Press, 1962.

———, *History of the United States Army*, New York: Macmillan, 1967.

———, *The American Way of War: A History of United States Military Strategy and Policy*, New York: Macmillan, 1973.

———, *History of the United States Army*, Bloomington, Ind.: Indiana University Press, 1984.

Wilson, Frederick T., *Federal Aid in Domestic Disturbances, 1787–1903*, New York: Arno Press, 1969.

Winders, Richard Bruce, *Mr. Polk's Army: The American Military Experience in the Mexican War*, College Station, Tex.: Texas A&M University Press, 1997.

———, *Panting for Glory: The Mississippi Rifles in the Mexican War*, College Station, Tex.: Texas A&M University Press, 2016a.

———, "Race and Republicanism: Understanding the Mindset of Mexican War Soldiers," in Geoffrey W. Jensen, ed., *The Routledge Handbook of the History of Race and the American Military*, New York: Routledge, 2016b.

Winthrop, William, *Military Law and Precedents*, Boston, Mass.: Little, Brown, and Company, 1896.

Woodward, C. Vann, "The Age of Reinterpretation," *American Historical Review*, Vol. 66, No. 1, October 1960.

Zelner, Kyle F., *A Rabble in Arms: Massachusetts Towns and Militiamen During King Philip's War*, New York: New York University Press, 2010.